My Life, My Story
The Odyssey Continues...

My Life, My Story
The Odyssey Continues...

A Memoir
Herbert Lawson, III

My Life, My Story
The Odyssey Continues...

© 2016 by Herbert Lawson, III

ISBN: 978-1-63110-254-7

Library of Congress Control Number: 2017943903

Photo Credits: Cover photo provided by:
Pop Nukoonrat and Josefkubes courtesy of Dreamstime.com
Author photos provided by Layne Photography

Printed in the United States of America by
Mira Digital Publishing
Chesterfield, Missouri 63005

Contents

Acknowledgements

I want to honor The Ancestors, Ase!

I do this for Mrs. Doris (The Great Mother).

I do this for Herbert Jr. (The Father).

I would like to thank my children Milan, Tehran, Kerstin and Elle; as well as KeyKey Davis for the book cover concept, thanks, Queen.

I also want to thank Layne Photography for the photoshoot, you guys are the best!

Lastly, I want to thank Muhammad Ali, Maurice White, Prince, and Korryn Gaines (The Warrior Princess).

Chapter 1

It's About Time

And at that time I knew I wasn't going up north but across the street to the main prison. Man! I had heard so much good shit about that place and I was ready, but there on the main yard it was another waiting period. You were put into this dorm (Cedar Hall) until you were classified. It wasn't that bad either. One advantage to me was we ate first, and the way they set us apart from the rest of the yard, we had to wear a green shirt instead of the prison blue. The classification process didn't last that long, maybe a week or two at the most, of course that didn't bother me. I just kept thinking, I've come this far and most of it was waiting, shit I could wait a little while longer. Finally, it's my time to go to where I'll be until I am eligible for parole. By now, I'm used to this shit. This might sound crazy, but I felt at peace as though I belonged. Man! I still remember walking to my dorm, niggas yelling — "What set you from cuz?" It's something about being a part of the crips family. It's a lot of crazy shit but on the flip side there's a lot of love too.

And as I entered the dorm, the first thing I saw was this pretty ass blonde with blue eyes CO fine as a motherfucker. Ms. Streans was her name. OH! I knew I had no chance, but just the thought of being around her did something to me. And besides I was all fucked up (you know with the shit bag and crutches) but I've always been a sucker for a pretty face. If nothing else I felt her being here kept me on my game with the women. Yes! I know I have a wife, but at some point all that married shit that makes a marriage work was gone. All I had come to know was money and getting high. So when I got here and I saw this beautiful woman, and it wasn't just her it was lots of beautiful CO's on this yard. For the first time in a long time I realized I was living in a lost and confused world of drugs and stupid shit because and the end of the day it came to nothing.

So I guess the thought of me being interested in her, made me see how much I've been missing out on in life. But that was not on the top of my list of shit to think about (you know what I mean) the first thing I needed to do was get adjusted to the yard and the shit that comes with it. Let me be honest I didn't know, but I did know this — prison and niggas would take advantage of you, and faster than a mother fucker. So my thing was just to look and listen while in Cedar Hall. The place where we came for the first week or two, niggas would come to the window and see if they had any homeboys and give you soap and other shit you might need, one reason they did this because upon coming to the main yard they (the CO's) take your shit away. So someone from Compton came by and hooked me up with some cosmetics and I don't remember who, but that's something everybody did for their people. Needless to say I did as well! This one cat — Bear Loc from Gardena, Ca. I befriended.

I don't remember how we met, maybe it was the guy who hooked me up when I was in Cedar Hall anyway he and I became close. I think that was the closest I've come to having a best friend since I was a kid. Bear Loc and I just clicked. The nigga was fearless and I didn't know him before meeting him here. I didn't know if any of the niggas from Compton had asked him to look for me or what. Well he became my right hand man. I don't know what the nigga saw in me. I wasn't your typical Crip. I didn't talk about all that gang shit. I mean I knew a lot of niggas from the dope game and gangsters, but I wasn't in to the banging part of it. I didn't like shit like killing niggas in a drive by. I made that known to Bear. Don't get me wrong I represented and respected that blue rag and I was true to it. You see it was no secret I was a Crip and Santa Fe Avenue in Compton was my spot. I'm on the main yard and shit is happening so fast you see shit would come your way whether you wanted it or not.

I was meeting all kinds of niggas, niggas from other dorms etc. See I was housed in the handicap dorm which was good, mainly because of my physical condition, besides we had all kinds of privileges that the other housing unit didn't or couldn't have. Dope was everywhere and money, liquor man, anything you wanted was here. Chino was everything and more than I thought it would be, it was unreal to be honest. It was better than the streets to some but fuck that there's nothing like being out on the streets. For me I just didn't want to like it like that. Unfortunately I met some who felt they needed to come back, but I didn't want that, I thought that was insane. Needless to say I was going to make the best of this stay. I was going to do my best to get out of here healthy and in my right mind. This is prison you can't take it for granted you just never know. I come to know shit could happen so fast around here. While in the reception center being locked down shit still jumped off.

So I didn't get the big picture of prison life, but I wasn't that naïve to think it was going to be that way here on the main yard. I had to be careful even with BearLoc at the beginning and besides that I wasn't looking to make friends. My focus was on getting healthy and getting my mind right. Everything else would be great but not needed. But as always for me shit seemed to come easy and prison would soon be no different.

Chapter 2

Game On

Cigarettes was and I'm sure still is as good as gold in the prison system, so it wasn't long before I got into the mix and before I knew it I was in deep. I linked up with this big as nigga who worked in the Chow Hall. Before I even met big dude, it was obvious my dorm was where you came to sell any and everything and just like on the streets some niggas would front you whatever. Niggas knew that Elm Hall was a gold mine and to have someone inside selling for them was a win- win situation and that's how I met Slim, this

Nigga was 6'11 300 pounds — shit I still remember the first time seeing him in the Chow Hall saying to myself why isn't this nigga playing football or basketball but then again I thought look at me I ain't shit either. Anyway, he was at the dorm selling some food. Well my wife was sending me money and the food in the Chow Hall wasn't worth the trip most of the time and often I was buying on the black market and sometimes I bought from him. So many times niggas and white boys would come to me for shit, shit like bread, etc. So one day I went to big dude about fronting me some bread and peanut butter and jelly thinking to myself shit that'll keep for a while and we would split it down the middle man! He agreed and we would soon have Elm Hall off the chain. At that point there's no doubt I would make it here in chino or in any other prison. It wasn't long before niggas was coming from every dorm looking for bread, peanut butter and jelly and even shit I didn't have.

At this moment it seems like I became the person I wanted to forget. But I couldn't the power of having people coming to you and hanging on to your every word is something I can't explain. This kind of power over people is not for man. Only God deserves that kind of power. Just like on the streets I wanted power it's no different in here. I wanted that power and I was good at getting it. I knew I wasn't God but I was searching for something and to be honest I didn't know who I was or what my life was about. The very thing I wanted to put behind me, while at the reception center, I honestly thought I was on my way to being that little boy who dreamed of being a star. But the gutter, the hood life it can be anything you want it to be. I guess that's what I wanted to be — a ghetto star. So I found myself getting so involved in this prison life and before long everyone knew my name. Shit was happening so fast that the CO chick came to me asking who are you and why are these guys jocking you like this. I would have loved to have been able to say some

Big ass dope dealer like freeway Rick or the cat's I worked for but that wasn't the case. I was nobody really (but I did know this) I was loving this and in here things were going my way but outside my wife and I were drifting apart. I knew that this was mainly my fault. One day I got a letter about some shit she was into with some woman who said she was having an affair with her husband and that if someone was to write me about it not to believe it, it isn't true. Well I felt like who would tell me that? I knew no one cared about me or my love life enough to give a shit about that. Then again I felt maybe this was a confession of some kind. After all I had done so much shit to her and payback is a motherfucker. To be honest I didn't give a shit but nevertheless we begin to write about this shit and it was becoming obvious she was a little uneasy with what was going on and maybe somewhat guilty. Meanwhile the little CO chick was getting friendly with me and flirting with me. In the beginning I played it off.

You see I had all kinds of issues that I was dealing with. The most important thing in my life at this point was to get the shit bag off my stomach and getting off of these crutches.

That would soon be happening. I had seen the doctor and he had gotten my medical records from Herman Hospital in Houston. He said he felt he could do the operation here at Chino Hospital. Frankly, I didn't care where he did it as long as it gets done. So that was my main concern not my wife or the CO chick. However, my wife was acting out of character and that was beginning to concern me. In the beginning I would get money, packages, whatever and about six (6) months into my prison stay she was changing. For example, I would call and check on her and the kid right before the lights would go out for count and for the first six (6) months she has never miss my call. The money would be here when she said and every quarter I would get a lil package. But now it's a different story.

Well, I would call on the weekend and she would be gone or no answer and I thought that was strange since the kid was so young and I felt she should be there after all the kid's just a few months old. After the first six (6) months not only did the money stop but the packages did too. It fucked me up because until now she had always been there. To be honest I had no idea what was going on. I thought maybe she's seeing someone but it was so early after the birth of our child. So I started thinking maybe she found out about Lori and whoever else. I knew niggas would begin to talk as soon as I went to prison. I decided the best thing to do was to just wait. If I've learned anything at all since I've been here is the one thing you cannot do is worry about shit like that, it'll drive you crazy. In the meantime I got all kinds of shit going on in here. First of all I've had the operation on my stomach to remove the bag, but not without some complication. The first operation seemed to have went well but after about three days of liquid I was given the ok to eat something solid.

Man! I had that thing on my stomach for so long it felt good no seeing it. I couldn't wait to eat. Not only could I not wait to eat, I was told I could eat whatever I wanted to eat. Being in prison I wanted a steak. Needless to say the doctor and I were looking forward to seeing what would happen, after all I had the shit bag on way to long because of my choosing to run from the law. Well in about thirty (30) minutes our worst fear became a reality. The steak, the potatoes and some green shit came back up. Needless to say I was scared. The doctor shared my pain and back into the operating room we went. This time the doctor felt that everything was going to be fine. After the second operation and the days of liquid it was time to eat something solid. I don't remember much about the meal (it damn sure wasn't' a steak) but just like the first time thirty (30) minutes later it all came back up. Put yourself in my place for a moment.

Here I am in a prison hospital and no one on the outside knows what's going on. I have to admit the doctors and nurses were the best. I could tell they were really concerned about me. Being in the hospital felt like I wasn't' in prison. In the hospital I was a person not just an inmate number. This was comforting and all but damn, what's wrong with me? Much to my surprise one of the nurses is sitting with me holding my hand telling me it's going to be ok. They have decided to send me to LOMA LINDA Medical Center. All I could think of was why I let this happen to me. Somehow I've got to pull myself together and let the doctor's do what they do. I knew the prison hospital wasn't the best and they are sending me out to a real hospital and having this nurse comforting me gave me some hope. Once I was at LOMA LINDA they ran all kinds of tests. Days passed by and finally some doctor came in to see me. He explained to me that because I wore the shit bag for longer than I should've and that caused some of the large colon to die.

This in turn had caused a blockage and that part of the large colon had to be removed. Of course I'm all for it, I just wanted to get better. Thanks God these doctor's got it right this time. After a few days I was back on the main yard again. It didn't take me long to get back on my feet. I fell right back into my routine — betting on all of the football games, basketball games, etc. you name it, I was into it. At this point my confidence was beginning to come back and that was exactly what I needed because before coming to prison I had lost all confidence in myself. I know what you are thinking — this is the most unlikely place to regain your confidence but hey it worked for me. It seemed like the right place at the right time for me, the shit bag and crutches were gone and I'm reading the Bible almost every day if not every day. Yet, I didn't turn to God for any kind of guidance. I just felt good reading His word more than any other books or magazines. I found the Bible fascinating but that was the extent of it. Hustling just seemed to be who I am.

Chapter 3

I'm Back

I embraced who I was — a hustler with my whole heart.
If I was unsure before about my future being on the main
yard and getting back my confidence. Now I know for sure I
have to give the game another shot. I knew my wife wanted
me to get a job and live a normal life and to be honest I
wanted that too at the time I told her that in letters while
in the reception center. But during the time I said those
things and felt that way I had no confidence in myself or my
hustle. At the time that seemed like the only thing I could
say. And maybe, just maybe her not knowing for sure what
I'll do was the reason for her running around doing dumb
shit. As I said before my wife and all her bullshit was just
gonna have to wait. I'm hustling again and that comes first.
Knowing that the game had beaten me up, I just wasn't one
to give up and being here on the main yard was just another
part of the game — One I felt I should take advantage of.
Still it wouldn't be without it's own bullshit. There's times
when the CO's would do their raids and I think they did our
dorm more than others.

Maybe they raided us more because of the privileges we had compared to the other dorms and on this night it was our time to be raided. I must admit I was warned by CO Stearns but as I often would do because she and I had gotten close. I was just like a love sick high school kid. I would get jealous when some ass kissing convict would go in and sit with her. I felt stupid when I caught myself feeling that way but she seems to encourage that kind of shit from me. On this night I wasn't' talking to her because of this. She worked second shift and when she had gotten to work that day she came by my bunk and told me to get rid of all the contraband I had. Being an asshole that day I wasn't trying to hear her and said fuck it and went back to what I was doing. That night at last count before her shift was to end here comes the raiding party and of course I was loaded down with all kinds of shit.

I had just got a shipment in from big dude early that day loafs of bread, peanut butter, jelly. Man! I had way too many packs of cigarettes. To be honest, I hadn't changed at all after spending all that time by myself in the reception center, reflecting on all that bullshit in my past, talking about changing, WOW! As soon as I got out of that place and on the main yard. I went back to the same shit as before, making bad decisions that always cost me some kind of problem that would hurt me. That's the kind of shit I wanted to rid myself of. I couldn't understand why I made these bad choices. Maybe I loved living on the edge of life. For me I guess it was feast or famine and no matter how hard I tried to change I would always come back to that old way of thinking. So the next day after they raided the dorm needless to say everybody knows. Hey, it's prison. Word gets out quick and when I saw Big Dude from the Chow Hall who was the supplier, I figured we would both take the loss and start over.

This is the state shit, after all. Besides I was the one who got the charge but I had a feeling that he would still want me to pay up in spite of what happen. Having this feeling he would try and punk me and I also knew the thing to do was to stand up to his big ass because by right we both lost out. This nigga thought that because he was 6'11 300lb. he could do what he want and in reality he could and I must have been crazy to even try to stand up to this big ass nigga. I felt I had no choice too many niggas looked up to me and besides that my nigga Bear Loc had my back, but still I was hoping since we both were Crips things wouldn't get to that point. Well I'm in the Chow Hall and I see big dude and as I was explaining to him what happened he basically stopped me and said, "Fuck that, you still owe me." Just like that. As

I said I wasn't going to let this nigga punk me. We had some words in the Chow Hall and I knew he wasn't going to do anything to me in there.

So he called me out saying it was going down on the weight pile. I knew many Crips on the yard but the only nigga I was close to was Bear Loc. After leaving the Chow Hall I went back to my dorm. As he did everyday Bear Loc came by and I told Bear Loc what went down not knowing what he would say and without hesitating Bear was ready to go to war with this fool. I knew he was for real and that's all I needed and I felt good about that. Well to my surprise all of the Crips I knew and the ones I didn't know came to my aid. GOD! I didn't know I had all this love so Bear Loc and the guys told me to meet him at the Weight Pile after he got off work and as far as he knew it was just me and Bear Loc and as we waited on the dude to get off work niggas was telling me, it's ok don't worry about shit we got this to be honest I didn't understand the love, maybe it was the crutch the bag was gone but I still had one crutch, maybe they didn't want to see me get fucked up. All I know is it made me feel good to have so many niggas standing with me.

Well! Here comes the nigga and he had a couple of niggas with him so when he came up to me and before he could say anything niggas was coming from everywhere, oh boy! I looked and I saw the same thing he saw and he began to sing a different song, but Bear Loc was saying cuz just say the word and I'll kill this nigga cuz. The big dude begin to say shit like I tried to talk to you Herb but you said you wasn't going to do shit. He was lying even though I knew big dude would have hurt me I couldn't let Bear Loc kill that nigga man! I didn't want any part of that kind of shit and after that night niggas was coming to me about all kinds of bullshit about this nigga about that nigga. After that night I was known on the yard, oddly enough I became one of the shot callers each race had one. I mean you had to have a shot caller. Someone has to represent their race the prison system couldn't exist without them, at least in California.

After that night I became the shot caller for the blacks and believe me when I say it was scary, it wasn't long before I would be tested. While chilling in my dorm, I was reading and listening to music and then suddenly I was called to the door and here was this Mexican shot caller and his boys. Apparently they had an issue with one of my people about a drug deal that had gone bad and while there's no shot caller school to go to and no one to confer with so the best and only thing to do was to pay the Mexicans what was owed to them and deal with that nigga later. After that was taken care of I went to Bear Loc (after all he is my right hand man) and explained to him what had happened. As always he would take care of it. You see I must admit I begin to feel like this shot caller nigga but deep down in my heart I didn't want this shit. This is prison and sometimes shit just comes your way whether you want it or not. I can truly say throughout my prison stay it was peaceful.

Somehow I felt I was on the right path and you sort of get used to the prison life, the people. And also I had this relationship going on with the CO, but man it's nothing like being free — free to come and go as you please. Sometimes while kicking back on my bunk I wanted to go home to my wife. She had given birth to our son. My future was looking bright I was healing inside and out I felt my confidence coming back but still I felt like the game owed me something not only that I had made up my mind about my future and that was to continue to sell dope. My wife had her own issues she was dealing with, you see this bitch had stooped to the point where she was asking me for money and I'm the one in prison. Nevertheless I felt I had to do it. After all I didn't know what was really going on down there in Louisiana. So I play the game with her maybe I know I was going to leave her when I came back. Besides I was having fun with the CO. She would call me in the office just to talk and ask me all kinds of questions about my life. I must admit I was somewhat surprised at the way she looked at me.

Chapter 4

Could it Be...?

Having the CO being really interested in me intrigued me. I didn't know if she was playing some prison game or what. To be honest I didn't know what to think about her. So I just played the game and at the end of the day I was feeling her. I recall her calling me in the office while she was eating strawberries and she was eating them in such a way that was so seductive saying to me Lawson the 3rd do you go in the back door? Now I'm all fucked up saying to myself why is she doing this shit to me? And at this moment game or not I'm playing too, I'm all in man. I found myself falling for this girl, besides it made me look at women for more than a piece of crack. If nothing else came of this that was something I needed to feel, before I got locked up I didn't feel anything. I'm beginning to feel good about myself and at every opportunity I tried to kiss and hold her and she kept telling me I want to kiss you too but we must wait.

We did get close a time or two but never long enough and that went on for a while pushing up on me and teasing me, I knew it was some kind of turn on for her. Maybe I'll never get the chance to really be with her but somewhere in the back of my mind I felt there's a chance. As my time was getting short and I begin to turn my focus to my wife and Ms. CO was listening to my phone calls. The more she listened the more I called and then I knew what I felt all the time, she did care you can't' fake jealousy. At this time I'm trying to get back to reality and to deal with my wife. The closer I got to getting out of prison the more I thought about my wife and what was going on with her. Maybe it was the truth that she was involved in a relationship with someone and it was nothing I could do to change that. This was just something I had to deal with. Nevertheless I was asking myself should I try and make it work or should I go on my way?

At the end of the day I felt the kid deserved a chance to have his dad. No doubt this was weighing heavy on my mind. It seemed the closer I got to going home the more involved the CO chick was getting with me. She was holding sex over my head saying things like, "Baby it's going down tonight," or "Maybe tomorrow night," but something would always come up. I thought we had several opportunities. She continued to tease me doing things like meeting me in the day room during count time because it was my job to clean the day room during count time. She was fucking with my head big time. I would go in the office and ask her to stop playing games with me but she would still do shit to fuck with me. Early on in the relationship hater's would go in the office hitting on her and when I felt comfortable talking to her, I went out on a limb and told her I didn't like that. Yes I know, who am I to ask such a thing but I did and to my surprise she enjoyed the jealousy I displayed. So to make matters worse she would only let them cats come in and sit and talk when I had pissed her off.

It seemed like the more I talked to my wife, the more she wanted to be around me. I told her I can't sit there and chit chat, it's just not what convicts do. She wasn't trying to hear that and I left the dorm for a while as soon as I would return there would be someone sitting in the office talking to her. Believe me she knew what that did to me. Most of the time I wouldn't let it bother me but it would be times when I played right into her hands and acted a fool. I've even went as far as to ask the convict to leave the office. It was clear to see that I had feeling for her and every convict knew it. As a matter of fact some of the CO's knew. Even when she worked with others she would call me into the office about dumb shit. The closer I got to going home the more she did it. BUT, at the end of the day going home meant everything to me. I had to check myself and separate myself from this prison life. Truth be told a part of me could have stayed in prison with her.

I had to be real and accept the fact that a relationship between me and the CO wasn't going to happen and that my wife was my reality. Soon I would have to face her and all her bullshit. Well months turned into weeks and weeks turned into days and I am looking forward to my release. I was concerned because i had gotten busted with the contraband and wasn't clear on whether or not they had added more time to my sentence. I knew for sure they had taken away my phone and store privileges for thirty (30) days but if I didn't do anything else maybe the thirty (30) days could be given back to me and needless to say I didn't get caught anymore. I had to check with my counselor and he told me that my release hadn't changed. Even though I had separated myself from the CO in the last remaining days but I really wanted to see her. but at the same time I was pulling away, someone had told her bosses how she felt about me . She felt that it was one of her co-workers. She wanted me to know that they had been fucking with her about us.

They couldn't prove that we were doing anything. So they just moved her around from dorm to dorm. After being told about this. I wanted more than anything to see her before I leave. However, that last week I didn't see her at all and now it's the night before my release no CO Stearns and it's clear to see I'm down when I should be full of joy but that wasn't the case. My heart was broken knowing what she was going through in these last days made me understand the position I had put her in. She could have been fired. If nothing else came out of this just knowing she cared made me feel good. I believed she cared from the very start. Knowing that I'm getting out in the morning I couldn't sleep and not being able to hear her voice made things worse. I laid down, turned on my headphones and fell into a deep trance. Out of nowhere here's this CO standing over me whispering to me, "Come to the office. " My heart began to race out of control.

The first thing that came to mind was I'm not getting out tomorrow. I kept my composure and put on my pants and went to the office. As I walked in the CO handed me the phone. I had no idea who it was or why they were calling me. To my surprise it was her and I must admit my heart was filled with joy. Before I could say anything she said don't talk just listen. I did just that. After listening to her I was ready to go out and take on the world. I have come a long way from shit bag and crutches to using the toilet and walking on my own. I was up early and ready to go, then it dawned on me, I didn't have a place to go to. My wife moved back to Louisiana and my brother was living in my old place with his girlfriend. I had no choice for the time being but to go back to my old place for the time being. I didn't see anything wrong with staying with him for a short time. Well things had changed in the sixteen (16) to twenty (20) months I had been locked up.

Chapter 5

My Brother, My Wife

My brother had come up with a hook up. He was moving lots of dope from Compton to Baton Rouge and as for my wife I wanted out but I wanted to see her and the kid. I also wanted to know the truth about what she was writing me about. I was the kind of nigga that if I thought you screwed someone while with me I didn't want you anymore. It was pretty much settled in my heart about her. How could I love her and trust her again? Nevertheless, I would send for her and my son. As far as my brother was concerned he and I didn't' always see eye to eye. There were moments when things were said that shouldn't have been and as brother we always would get through it. However, my main concern was to get back to Louisiana. Convincing my parole officer would turn out to be one hell of a task. It seemed that he knew my intention it was somewhat scary because he was telling me what I was thinking.

No matter what he says I'm doing what I want to do. Fuck him! Well he couldn't stop me from going, but it was going to be a thirty (30) day wait before I would leave. I didn't have to take a drug test as far as I knew. I was glad because my brother had some bad ass weed. I'm not much of a weed smoker but one night I rolled me a joint of that shit and before I got halfway through I was all fucked up. I started tripping on shit like what if my parole officer came in on me smoking this shit. Needless to say I didn't want anything to do with that. Well my parole officer didn't come over and I slept off my high. I'm looking forward to seeing my son. He was born while I was in prison and that was the only thing that could've kept me from being there when he was born. I was determined not to treat him like I did his brother. I had to deal with the fact that I was just like my dad. I think knowing that I think might have made me turn to drugs and drinking.

I had become the very person I wanted to hate and never wanted to become like. I think at that point I was beginning to understand who my dad was. I had to look inside of me and try and understand why I did what I did. My dad wasn't there for me and I had come to know that my dad's dad wasn't there for him and I think at that moment I stopped being angry with him. As they say the apple don't fall far from the tree. It's a little too late thinking about that. It wasn't going to do me any good now. I had only one thing on my mind and that was to go back to Port Allen and take back my block. The dope game is what I've come to love and I felt that's where I belong. So I just have to get through these thirty (30) days and make peace with my brother if I was going to win. To be honest I was out of line to be angry with him because if he had some issues with me he had every right.

When he had came to Compton I hadn't taken care of him or any of my other family members like I should have and if he felt I needed to humble myself I was smart enough to know and accept that. Besides he was my way back to where I wanted to be and I must admit my brother was winning. Those guys had always forgiven me in the past for the silly shit I would do to them. So my brother and I had put all the bullshit behind us and we had a plan in place. When I got back to Louisiana all it is now is for my parole officer to let me go. In the meantime my wife is coming out here. Who knows maybe it'll be different when I see her. When she arrived it was all bad and I didn't realize that I had so much anger towards her. First of all I felt betrayed and it really hit me when I picked her up from the airport and I saw her differently. Maybe I should have just waited for her to tell me what had went on but I started with the bullshit right off the bat.

No matter what had happened I should have been more forgiving after all. I had done so much fucking up I was the one who was unfaithful first, but as I said before I had become my dad. He was selfish and so was I. I felt I could do whatever I wanted and with no consequences. I know that's not reality but that was the way I saw it. I wasn't seeing her side of things because all I saw was her betraying my love. I guess when you're selfish you only look at things one way and because of my way of thinking it was over between us. She stayed a few days and to be honest she tried her very best to get me to see her side of things or just put it behind us. It was no use. I was done with her and for me the next and only thing to do was to say goodbye and back to Louisiana she went with the baby in tow. I just wanted the marriage to be over after all no more shit bag, no crutches. I felt like a new man. I didn't need her ass anyway who does she think she is to fuck around on me. Honestly in those remaining days in prison I really tried to understand her reason for doing what she did but when I got out I couldn't do it because I measured women by my mother. My mother would never have done that to my dad that's how I saw it. Well my thirty (30) days of waiting was finally over and needless to say I can't wait to go get the paper from my parole officer. As before he tried to talk me out of going by telling me all the shit I was going to get into in Louisiana and he was right but I was determined to go. I had been waiting for this moment since the accident. To me this was just like being raised from the dead, another victory. My brother and I had come up with a plan. We figured I would go down to Louisiana first and then he would come down a day or two later. Before I leave Los Angeles, I just have to try and get with the CO and one night I got drunk and decided to call the prison.

Not knowing if I would get through to her, and to my surprise I did and we talked. Damn! I tried my best to convince her to meet me somewhere but as always she had some excuse but there was hope because she took my phone number and I should have left it up to her but I got drunk again and called but this time someone else answered the phone in the dorm and I think he recognized my voice and began to ask my name, I hung up and that was the end of that. Now I'm ready to go, parole papers in order, ticket in hand — Louisiana here I come. I feel good about my future.

Chapter 6

Back in the Game!

Well I'm here in Port Allen. It looks just like before. My brother must have come the same day I did because the next day he called. I met him to get my dope. I was a little surprised I didn't think it would be this soon. Come on, the next day? I was overjoyed. My brother felt he needed to talk to me about how things had changed since I had been gone. As usual I didn't want to hear anything.

I was going to do this my way, so while he was talking in my mind I was just thinking about how much I wanted to start with. One other thing I thought about at this point was how good my brother was to me in spite of how I treated him and the others. He had a key of cocaine waiting for me, so we decided on 9 ounces to start. There was no doubt in my mind that I was on my way to the top. When I had gotten the dope I knew all I had to do was go by the Quick "N" Handy store and let them niggas know I was back and in business. Before I could get to my mother's house niggas was coming. My sister — Bay and I was the only two at the house at this time. My mom was at work; my wife had come by with the baby asking for money. I had just made two sales of about $2,000.00 dollars and I told her to fuck off. Shit was happening just that fast another 2 sales niggas are coming and I hadn't even bagged up any of the dope. Finally it slowed down and I'm bagging up some dope.

I have the music playing loud, snorting some coke and feeling good as a motherfucker. All of a sudden through all of the loud music my sister was knocking on the door yelling for me to open the door and before I could turn down the music it was too late. The police was kicking in the door. It was a like a bad dream. It was happening so fast that it didn't seem real, but it was real and to make matters worse the dope was in plain view, I didn't have a chance I was busted and as far as I was concerned it was an open and shut case. I knew the cops must have said the same thing and the first thing that came to mind was who ratted me out but at the end of the day it didn't matter. I was busted. I couldn't help but think about what my brother tried to tell me and I thought I knew the people I had served that day because these people had been in the game a long time but things had changed. Unfortunately I had to see for myself and it cost me again that day.

I'm desperate now to the point where I had the nerves to ask my sister to take this charge for me. I know that's crazy (but what's even crazier I believed that she might do it.) But as they say desperate people do desperate things. Like any sane person she said, "No, Hell no!" I had the nerve to be disappointed in her but I understood. We both were taken to jail. I guess just because she was in the house they took us both to jail. It wasn't long before they would let her go home and I knew it was real. In my mind I had no way of getting out of this one. To add insult to injury my wife came to the jail to tell me how much she hated me and I was such a fool and that she was divorcing me. I'll admit that she wasn't on the top of the list for shit to worry about right now. I had just got out of prison thirty (30) days ago and now here I am in jail again caught in the very act with the dope. The only thing I could think of was God and you got to help me.

I know we all say that when we come to jail, but He's all you got at this point and I had read the Bible in prison and it was always a peace that come over me reading the Bible. That's something I'm going to need going through this shit you see this wasn't California this is Louisiana they will throw your ass away here for bullshit and here I am with ounces of cocaine, they were already sending word to me about taking thirty (30) years. I had nowhere to turn but I thought back to my childhood when I would talk to God whom I couldn't see but I could feel and he was always there for me. Maybe I could call on him or maybe I was just a little kid and all that stuff was in my mind besides so much time had passed and I had went on to believing in just myself. I need to know, I need to see if it was God and if it was God maybe He'll help me. So while I'm getting booked I began to cry out in my heart and to my surprise the first thing I see when I got to a cell was this white cover Bible and needless to say I took a hold of that Bible as if my life depended on it and it really did as far as I was concerned and when I picked up that Bible I knew I was getting out of this somehow. I just knew inside of me something would happen for the good. I mean I didn't call myself a Christian or anything like that but I just knew because it was the same voice I used to hear and talk to as a child back in Sunrise and Port Allen. Maybe back then I didn't understand who I was talking to or why but he was real and I could hear his voice as if it was my father. He was everything to me. At the same time I still have to deal with these white folks and that was one thing that I knew for sure. It wasn't too many people willing to help me. I wasn't going to fool myself at least I knew that. Another thing I had going for me, in here I knew everybody. My cousin Eric was in the same cell along

with my childhood friend Duke Murphy from Ave. B in
Port Allen.

It was crazy in here as you'll see throughout this Chapter.
First thing I want to do is talk about one of the jailers.
Roebe was this old white man who I had come to respect
and like. Roebe thought that I was some kind of Drug King
Pin. Maybe he felt because I was on parole from California
and they had a hold on me and on top of that you got niggas
calling me the Governor. That kind of shit really had him
going. I think with all that he had this perception of me
that was bigger than who I really was but whom I wanted
to be. Roebe and I went at it all the time but it was all good.
Then there was Henry he was real laid back and he would
do anything to make the inmates comfortable and shit like
that was unheard of in Los Angeles County Jail and we
didn't give him any trouble. There's another jailer I want to
mention and that's Fred. He was one cool ass brother. He
would let us get drinks and cocaine, weed etc. By now the
days were turning into weeks and nothing is happening
concerning my case and do you want to know something?
I'm feeling nothing at all. I'm at peace with the situation.

I was at peace with the whole situation. At this time Lori
had started coming to see me. After all she was one of the

reasons my wife did what she did. I don't know that for sure and I didn't see anything wrong with Lori coming to my aid now. Matter of fact I needed her. Besides that she was bringing me food, liquor and whatever. My family was never the ones I depended on when I went to jail or prison. Besides Lori made me feel good about myself. She still saw me as the person I had been before I left to go to California. She was there when I needed someone. Having my cousin Eric, my boy Duke Murphy and others it just didn't seem like I was facing thirty (30) years but it was real and no matter how much liquor, dope, etc. I was facing a lot more than I could bear myself. So I started looking at ways of escaping out of here. It was a long shot but what did I have to lose at this point? So I began to recruit niggas to help me but I had to be careful about the people I shared my thoughts with.

I also fell deep into that Bible and I truly felt that it would have to be something supernatural. It's strange the way things were happening. It was this dude that they had put in our cell block, he was from south Baton Rouge. His name was Larry. Larry had been listening to my situation and I guess he heard the hopelessness in my talk, etc. One day I was up early and just thinking about how I'm going to get out of here and while sitting at the table reading and thinking here comes Larry. He tells me about his mother and that his mother had a friend who was a prophet. To be honest I knew nothing about what a prophet was or anything like that. He began to tell me some things she had done to help him get out of. At this point it wasn't gonna take too much to convince me to at least talk to her or anyone else who could help me. I was willing to try almost anything but I must admit I didn't want to play with any kind of witch craft so I had to give this shit a lot of thought. I didn't want God angry with me.

It's already like I've got the whole world pissed off at me and having God pissed off with me I know I wouldn't have a chance. The next day these Christian people came in to pray with us and Mrs. Morgan called me to her and said that I had the spirit of some guy in the Bible named Joseph on me. That really fucked me up. I mean I'm reading the Bible at this time and Larry's telling me about this prophet and here comes Mrs. Morgan talking about this spirit of Joseph. Man, my head is smoking right now. When she said this about me and as soon as they had prayed and left I couldn't wait to read about this Joseph. There was no great awakening inside of me after reading his story. I must admit I was looking for a sign or something but I didn't understand the Bible either and I was angry at God because of my lack of understanding of His book. However, something inside of me wanted to keep reading and I did. While reading my mind was wondering all over the place thinking.

Here I am with this new dope charge here in Port Allen knowing that these fuckers could and would throw me away and I didn't know how parole worked in California. Would California just let me be done with parole and turn me over to Port Allen? There's so much going on in my mind and every time I would ask someone it got worse with every answer. So I turned my attention to escaping out of here more and more. Now all I need is someone on the outside to help me and as it were there was so many people coming to visit. I felt my chances were good that I would find someone to help me. I was getting worried you see weeks were turning into months and to make matters worse I wasn't hearing anything from the DA. The only time they had said something was when he had told my mother about the thirty (30) years. Other than that nothing had been said. So in my mind, unless God came through the only thing to do was escape.

I knew my chances of escaping was slim to none. Nevertheless I had hope in what that prophetess had said to me. She had told me to read these chapters of Psalms at the same time every day and if I did exactly what she said I would walk out of here. This was like one of those Bible stories I was reading. I applied just what she said and it became a part of my daily routine. In the meantime I had my brother sending me drinks and drugs etc. and Lori was bringing me food to eat. Yes I felt the love but it was no substitute for freedom. I was still facing a lifetime in prison. Having the drinks the drugs and the food eased the pain even if it was only for a moment. I had also gotten this big ass radio and on weekends we would blast the hell out of that radio. Being drunk, I did the coke once and I found that being high on that cocaine in a cell wasn't for me. It made me feel trapped like a lion in a cage of some kind. So the coke was for the other guys.

That's something that I would never do again, that was worse than being locked up in jail. I've done a lot of stupid shit and I felt bad about it but nothing I've done made me feel like that and believe me I've had a lot of shameful moments, but doing coke in jail was the lowest. I continued to drink and the thought of doing thirty (30) years in prison outweighed the high I got from the alcohol. Eric and Duke made it bearable but I have to get out of here. If doing the drinking and the drugs did anything for me, it took me to a place I didn't want to go. For some strange reason it took me to my reality. Something I will have to face one day. Maybe I thought I could drink and one day I'll be out of here (who knows what I was thinking). One thing I knew for sure was I needed a miracle and also I needed to sober up to figure out what I needed to do about getting out of here. As I sobered up I kept reading the Psalm the prophetess gave me. At this point it was my only hope. Every nigga in the jail just knew I was going down for a long time. It felt scary knowing that these niggas thought they would be looking at me for the last time. Something inside of me wouldn't and couldn't accept that.

Chapter 7

Is This Really Happening To Me?

To make matters worse I found myself getting sick. There was a sharp pain in my side. This was something that caught me by surprise and it hurt so badly. At times it was hard to walk. I tried to wait and see if it would pass in a day or two but it only got worse. One night I was unable to stand upright and then I had no choice but to go to the doctor. I was taken to the emergency room at Earl K. Long hospital. The doctors didn't do much for me nor did they tell me what might be wrong. Maybe once they found out what I was in jail for maybe the doctors thought I just wanted to get some pain pills or something. Thank God the pain had somehow eased a little bit.

I'll admit when I got to the hospital I was better I thought it was strange because all day I was in so much pain. I thought maybe I'm going crazy. Could it be the stress of facing thirty (30) years? I didn't know nor did I understand. The next day I was back into a fetal position from the pain. Within minutes I was calling for the jailers and I was taken back to the ER at Earl K. Long. Just as the day before I couldn't even stand upright because of the pain. This was a different doctor and he knew I was hurting but he couldn't see what was wrong. He told me that every Wednesday they had a specialist come in and look at patients in my condition. The doctor gave me a shot and made an appointment for me to see the specialist. I was very shocked that the jail was ok with the whole thing. Truth be told they had no choice because the doctor had confirmed that something was wrong and I needed to see a specialist. I was in pain all the time and it was obvious I wasn't faking.

After he gave me that shot I felt so much better but in the morning I was doubled over in pain again. Thank God it's Tuesday and Wednesday is near. I was able to bear the pain by just lying there in that fetal position. First thing Wednesday morning I was up and ready to go. As I often do in the morning, I started my day reading my bible and it wasn't long before it was time to go. As we sat and waited to see the specialist the nurse came in to ask me some questions. She also wanted to take x-rays that required me to drink some type of special dye that would allow them to look at areas in my mid-section. After looking at the x-rays the doctor in charge informed me that I had a kidney stone. They told me I needed to be taken to New Orleans as soon as possible because they didn't have the necessary facilities

at Earl K. Long to treat me. The sheriff department had
no problem with me going to New Orleans and of course I
would be going with a deputy sheriff.

Officer Roebe got the job of taking me to New Orleans. I
think deep down Roebe liked me. He had this picture of
me being this big drug dealer nigga from California who
came to Port Allen and was gonna make Port Allen like
Los Angeles. There was some truth to what he thought.
However the reality was different in that I wasn't from
California but he just couldn't believe that. Maybe he just
wanted to believe his version either way it was alright
with me. At the jail I acted like I was some drug King Pin.
He and I went at each other all the time and he enjoyed
it just as much as I did. My stay in the Port Allen Jail was
an experience I would never forget. They treated me
differently from the other inmates. Possibly because like
Roebe they all thought I was some big time dope dealer and
we have him. They gave me too much credit and I played it
for all that it was worth.

I could tell Roebe was excited about the trip to New Orleans
and something struck me as odd. I thought I was wearing
my orange jumpsuit all though we didn't have to wear it in
the jail but this was different we were going to New Orleans

and yet the sheriff said it was ok to wear street clothes. It really didn't matter to me one way or another since I'll be going to the jail ward at the hospital but it just seemed odd. On the hour and a half ride to New Orleans Roebe managed to make a stop and got himself and me something to eat and drink. Upon arriving at the hospital I knew nothing about it other than I was born there. Roebe didn't have a clue as to what to do next. I guess he never did this before. I'm not going to help him at all on this one. I like him and all but I wanted to see how this would unfold. I saw an opening here and I wanted to just play it out.

I thought the hospital had a plan in place because I was in custody and they know this I'm sure the doctor had done all the paperwork needed but I was hopeful and maybe you can imagine what my thoughts were. After hours of waiting and finally getting checked in I thought I was going to the jail ward and you often do when you are in custody or maybe I'll get a room and Roebe would stay with me, but soon after I checked in Roebe took off. After waiting for thirty (30) minutes which turned into two hours for Roebe to return, I still don't have a room and I am being treated like any other patient. I thought he had gone to the office about keeping me in the jail ward or something but that wasn't' the case. This fucker was gone. I mean, gone back to

Port Allen. So I just sat there and waited for my room. I am confused here because I am thinking to myself this can't be happening. This guy left me here and while I am in shock I am also thinking this is the chance I've been hoping and waiting for.

First I need to get the stone taken care of. I had gone through this kind of shit before with the shit bag and the crutches. Besides I wasn't quite sure what was really happening here. It all happened so fast and unexpectedly. I just have to wait and see it through. The staff has noticed that Roebe has not come back and they are asking me where is he? I don't have an answer nor do I care because this is what I want. So the nurses call the administrator who was also baffled about the whole thing as well. The day was almost over and here come the administrator. She said she had no authority to put me in the jail ward. She told me that she was going to call the sheriff and see what he wanted her to do and would be back to tell me what he said. Of course that was the last thing I wanted her to do, but it was out of my control. She returned with a strange look on her face, I couldn't figure it out. To my surprise she said the sheriff wasn't concerned about me at all and he wasn't sending anybody back here to be with me. He told her if he leaves, he leaves and if I came back that was up to me. As far as she was concerned I was a free man and his response was so be it. After meeting with her I received my bed. In the morning I saw my doctor and was told the process he wanted to use and that he thought it would be about a week to complete. In the course of this week I could piss it out and if not then some kind of surgery would have to be done. After meeting with the doctor I was in disbelief and the first thing I did was call my mom to tell her everything that has happened. My head and my heart was on a crash course. I didn't know what to think or what she was going to say. After telling her what had happened I couldn't hear nothing she said. My mind was somewhere else. All I heard was escape over and over in my head. I don't need to ask her about running because I was doing that regardless. I guess I wasn't looking for her permission I wanted her love. I just wanted her to love me.

Also, I had to go before God about what has happened. I knew I have to be real with him. I also knew God wouldn't bless wrong doing, but I prayed before him anyway. To be honest I knew God would help me. At the end of my talk with my mom she said make sure I get the kidney stone taken care of. To me that was her blessing; her way of telling me to go and be careful. I got the treatment I needed and at the end of the week the stone had disappeared. No

kidney stone, no surgery and now I needed to wait on the
doctor to release me. Boy, my head is really going now. So
many thoughts — are they coming? Should I leave now?
Where do I get the money? Where do I go from here? You
name it I thought about it. There was one thing I knew for
sure and that was I can't go back to Port Allen. That would
be an insane act but I was known to do some pretty insane
things. With this in mind, Baton Rouge wasn't out of the
question because if I limited the people I saw I could pull it
off and I could stay in Baton Rouge until I figured it all out.

I have to calm down and let this all play out . I could be
released and the Port Allen sheriff could still come to pick
me up. The night before I was released I had a chance
to meet my dad's half-brother for the first time. My
grandfather also came to visit a couple of times as well.
That night I had all kinds of things to reflect on. I didn't tell
my uncle what I was planning on doing but I did tell my
dad and my grandfather because I needed to stay at my
grandfather's. I could tell my grandfather wasn't too keen
on the idea but I was his grandson and besides it was only
for one night. The doctor finally came in and said everything
was alright and I could go. I called my grandfather to pick
me up and while I was waiting I wondered who would show
up first — the sheriff or my grandfather. My grandfather

showed up first. I could tell he was a little uneasy with the idea and I truly understood. He's normally a fun guy to be around but this situation made it odd for us and I understood that, but as usual it's about me being selfish just worrying about myself.

To me it was only for one night. I had a chance to meet his girlfriend. She was very nice and much younger. Even though this was a difficult situation to have put him in, I still enjoyed being with him. Little did I know this would be the last time I would see him alive because he died while I was on the run. The next day my mother sent my cousin Jackie to come and get me. Jackie lived in Baton Rouge and it was perfect. I would stay with her and to my surprise my mom had gotten the whole family in on helping me. I needed that because I felt so alone. I felt this way mostly because of the choices I made. I couldn't blame anyone. I knew god had his hand on this and to what extent that I didn't know. One thing I did know I wasn't ready to give up my lifestyle. This shit just added to all the crazy shit I've done.

When I got to Jackie's house all kinds of niggas was coming by giving me advice or whatever. They were big on giving advice and short on giving money. I appreciated the advice but I needed money right now. I know to most of these niggas my life was like a movie. Knowing some of them was thinking this might be the last time they will see me again. Honestly I had got caught with a lot of dope and I had just gotten out of prison. In the past I loved that circus atmosphere. I clearly understand how people saw me and even I wanted to see what happened next. For some reason I enjoyed watching my life being played out in public, in spite of my fears. After a few days of freedom it didn't bother me who knew where I was, all I wanted was to see Lori. She had done so much for me and I wanted to see her and tell her how thankful I was. I knew I only had a few days at the most to get out of town before the police would know where I was. So I wanted to make the most of the time I had.

Well it didn't take much to get her over to where I'm staying but I knew she would be somewhat shocked. As far as she was concerned I wasn't getting out anytime soon. So when I called her and asked her to come see me, she thought she was going to pick up something and bring it to me at the jail. When I told her, "I'm out and at my cousin's house waiting on you," she dropped the phone and came over. I got what I could from her. She didn't have much but she was young and fine. Plus, the sex was good and that's all I wanted because I couldn't take her with me. Besides,

Wanda had found out about my great escape and I guess she had a change of heart or maybe she called herself having pity on me. She wanted me to know that she was doing her wifely duties and she also told me she was still in love with me. I didn't know if I believed her or not, I really didn't care. My concern now was beyond my marriage. My marriage problem seemed like a tiny speck compared to what I have going on now.

The moment I got out of that hospital my focus became where I'm going to get money from? Where am I going to live? And last but not least what's my name going to be? How am I going to get to wherever I'm going? So with all this shit going on in my head all my wife could do for me at this point is help me with money. I needed lots of help in that department. I played along with her and asked her to come with me. She said she was scared and I understood but I wanted her to know it could work out. I told her maybe I could go a year and get caught or maybe I could go forever without getting caught. I think in her mind I was just full of shit and just thinking about myself and actually that is the case. To me it was possible very possible that this could all work out. I am reading the Bible and to be honest I still didn't understand it for the most part but I believed it. I felt if those stories were true about Joseph and Moses maybe God will show himself to me. Getting out of that jail was not supposed to happen. That had to be God. I'm not a Christian, I just went to church as a kid, but I felt he heard my request and I'm not going to deny what I feel.

I felt guilty asking God to be with me in this mess but on the inside I felt like HE was all I had. It was a strange feeling inside I had faith in him. On the outside I was this dope dealing motherfucker. I was very torn. When I wasn't seeing Lori I was trying to convince Wanda that we could have this wonderful life somewhere but where? That part I hadn't figured out yet. In my eyes all she had to do was love me and trust me but that was hard to sell to her. All she had to do was remember our situation a few months back, so if she didn't come with me I understood. After a lot of begging, although she was scared, she decided to come with me. She had conditions though. She wasn't coming until I was there (wherever there was) and I had a job and a place. Then and only then would she come. I didn't know if I believe her or not. At this point I didn't have a choice. At this point she had taken a lot of bullshit from me and I was really surprised she was even considering getting back with me. I needed to leave soon and my wife didn't have any money but she gave me what she did have — food stamps. As simple as this was it meant something to me, she gave me what she had. She didn't have to do it and something inside of me wanted to work it out.

The question was could I forget about the nigga she had been with when I was in prison. I knew she did what she did because of what I had become. But, just like every other nigga I knew I was selfish. I really believed that no matter what I did she was supposed to honor me no matter what! That's how I saw it. The big question is can I forgive and forget? Right now my love life will have to wait.

It's time for the last phase of the great escape — getting out of town. I stayed with Jackie about a week or so. She was great but I couldn't stay here any longer not knowing if I was a wanted man or not. I had to get out of town, but I had very little money and it was more than obvious at this point that I wasn't going to get much more help from niggas. I had done a lot with little before and this would be no different.

Chapter 8

Bus Station Please

I said my goodbyes went to the bus station. I scrapped up enough money to buy a ticket to anywhere in the United States. So where to? Well California was out of the question since I was still in the legal system there and chances are I would have gotten busted real quickly, but I still wanted to go west. As a little kid in school I loved history and geography. Because of this I developed an interest in moving out west. In my mind it was as far away as I could get from Louisiana. So should I go to Denver, Seattle or Portland? Hummm....Decisions.... Well I decided to go to Denver.

Upon arriving in Denver unfortunately for me it was winter. I had very little money so keeping warm was a challenge. Fortunately for me, I befriended a chick who was on her way to Seattle. On the ride to Denver we talked. She told me how she had been on vacation in the south and was on her way back home and I told her how I was looking for a place to settle down and start over because my marriage hadn't worked out (well I didn't totally lie). She began to tell me about Seattle and listening to her it seemed like a place I could go and blend right in. I took in everything she said but I still chose to go to Denver. As we pulled into Denver all I could see was snow. It didn't faze me at all until the night air hit me. Damn! It's cold as a motherfucker out here.

As I got off the bus immediately I had second thoughts. So I got back on the bus in the morning and asked the young lady to tell me more about Seattle. During the layover she began to tell me about the shelters, food outlets and different food programs they have for the homeless. As she was talking I was thinking this might be the better choice. The only downside was that she told me it rains a lot. That didn't seem too bad. I mean it rains a lot in Louisiana. It can't be that bad. Well I would come to learn that it really rains in Seattle. I mean really rains. Sometimes for weeks at a time without stopping.

Seattle turned out to be everything she said it was and more. There were lots of homeless people and runaways all over downtown and more to the point there were lots of places to find food and shelter. I fit right in and that was exactly what I needed to do. The last thing I needed was to stand out. I needed to go underground and unlike what I did in Los Angeles instead of using a bunch of fake names I wanted a new identity. I didn't care if I lived under that new identity for the rest of my life. At least I would be free.

My first few days in Seattle I flowed with the crowd. It kind of reminded me of the Hippie Movement in San Francisco. This was a place where everybody was either looking for something or running from something. Everyone was in their own world. I remember my first night I stopped by some musicians and they were playing with such passion I just stood there listening. Then I started dancing and before I knew it I decided to help myself to the congas and I began playing with them. Before long there was this crown of people who gathered watching and dancing as well. That night all of my fears were gone. I had no thoughts of the police or being in jail. This feeling was something that I had not experienced in a while. That night I realized that for a long time my life had been filled with so much bullshit. Drugs, police, alcohol, sex. I realized I had been trapped inside myself. I was my own worst enemy. That was more frightening to me than the thought of prison. The question was how could I escape myself? I often battled with myself. There was a war going on inside of me and it was a war I didn't know if I could win.

My future didn't look too bright at this point. So I took a
roll at the dice. I took on the name Jamie Johnson. Things
started to change for me once I changed my identity. I didn't
care to drink much at all anymore. I think I began to realize
how important my freedom was. That night of playing
the congas and feeling free felt like a turning point in my
life. Well had I really changed? In true fashion I used the
musicians whom I found out were brother and sister for
what I needed that night. I slept with the sister and in the
morning returned to my reality.

I needed to find a good shelter so that evening I found a
bed. The next thing for me was a job. So once I was settled
in the shelter I started asking around about jobs. I was told
about this car wash where a lot of homeless guys would go
to get work. They would pay you the same day. Someone
said it was down by the King Dome. I went to sleep feeling
good knowing that I had a place to sleep, three (3) meals
a day and tomorrow would bring the opportunity of a job
that paid daily. I was so thankful that I didn't have to sleep
on the streets. The next day I made my way to the car wash
and everything worked out just as the people at the shelter
said. Rob the manager at the carwash was a cool guy and he
hired me right on the spot.

Rob was the kind of person who just cared about people. As I looked around that car wash there were people from all walks of life. Black, white, Hispanic it didn't matter, Rob just cared about people. Knowing this made me want to be there. He didn't ask me anything about where I was from before he hired me. He only asked me my name. Working at the car wash worked out perfect because I didn't need any ID and I was paid in cash daily.

Most of the guys who worked there were alcoholics and dope fiends so they didn't work full time and only showed up one to three days out of the week. The only people there all the time were Rob (the manager), Phyllis (the cashier), Jodie (the part time cashier) and Lenny — he did most of the detail work. There are few regulars. One by the name of Darren, the service writer, had only been there a month or two. He and I got along well and sometimes he would come and take me away from downtown. I need that. Being in the shelter felt like a halfway house. Don't get me wrong I was happy to have a roof over my head, but I knew I deserved better and I was determined to get out of that shelter. I thanked God for the shelter and the food there even though it sucked and besides with the job I could go out and buy my own dinner. Now that I was working it was just a matter of time before i would be out of there.

I stayed at the carwash all day every day. My first assignment was to vacuum out the cars then I moved up to drying off cars and putting Armor All on tires. I wanted to be the best there and I worked hard at it. The tips were coming in but I wanted more so I began selling more services like wax jobs to customers. This turned out great for Darren because he would get a percentage of the sale. It turned out to be good for me as well because I worked quickly and did it well. This turned in to more tips, bigger tips for me. Rob also noticed how good I was at this car wash shit.

Rob began to ease me in as a service writer. At first I said no way. First of all I knew nothing about the business and secondly I didn't want to step on anybody's toes. I was new to these guys. I didn't want to call attention to myself. I was just hustling trying to make more tips. I was good with the way things were After thinking about things Rob was giving me a chance and I should be thankful. How could I say no? And really it wasn't that hard to me. It was like selling dope. Just selling the products and i knew I was good at that. I just used the same principle I used when I sold dope. When someone came into the carwash I was going to sell something to you whether you wanted it or not and in the process build a relationship so you would come back again.

With this new opportunity the most important thing for me at this point was to stay drug free. My freedom depended on it. New identity or not the charges in Louisiana were still there and no matter how well things were going here I had to be very careful. Having a new identity gave me a chance new life but the reality was I still had an old identity that I couldn't' forget and there was nothing I could do about it.

I knew I was one high away from going back to jail so being drug fee was a priority. It didn't take me long to embrace the service writer's job. I just thought of it as another hustle. It wasn't long before I was the number one service writer not just for the location where I worked but for the company. There were locations all over, one near the Space Needle and another in Tacoma. My sales surpassed everyone else. Rob, Phyllis and I became closer this was nice and surprising in a way because I thought Phyllis didn't like me. I guess she just had to see what kind of person I was. So many people came through that place that you didn't know who was real or fake. This made it hard for her to take anyone who worked there seriously. Face it most of us came from the shelter and were probably running from something in our past.

The closer we all became she started to open up to me. I tried to be as normal as possible and for the most part I was doing a good job pulling it off on the outside, yet On the inside I was struggling. I had run from the law before but this is some serious shit. Making it here is the difference between freedom and a thirty (30) year sentence. In the many previous brushes with the law there was always hope but this time was different. I wanted and I needed the name Jamie Johnson and the identity I was building to work. I spent every chance I got trying to make it a legal name but identity theft had become such a problem in the United States that it made it almost impossible to do.

I just decided to keep a low profile. I was making enough money now as service writer to move out of the shelter. I was by no means rushing but I had put in my time. I had been there for weeks now but it was too soon for an apartment and believe me the money I was making wasn't that great. But, it was good enough for me to move into one of the run down hotel's downtown. This was perfect for me. It kept me close enough that I could still walk to work. It wasn't the Hilton but it was cheap and clean and it was better than the shelter. I thought, man I'm on my way now. I started getting out more. I went to baseball games because the car wash gave us the tickets due to sales being the best they had ever been and to top it off I loved baseball. The New York Yankee's were my favorite team and Seattle's team really wasn't that good but it was free and I enjoyed the games. Sometimes I went with Jodie or Darren but most of the time I went alone. I used the time to reflect on my life. My mind would always take me back to my wife and my kids. Maybe just maybe everything would work out here and we could be a family. The family she always wanted.

I spoke with her and I gave her the real. I didn't know how long things would last. I could go twenty (20) years and not be caught or that knock at the door could come in two (2) days. I didn't know. What I did know and what I told her was it would be hard for her. Well she was focused on us being a family and decided she was willing to come out and check out the situation. I was excited about her coming and bringing the kid. Everyone at the car wash knew how excited I was. Seattle just felt right. I knew she would love it if she could just keep her mind on living this new life and not the old one I was trying to leave behind. I knew this was a lot to ask of her but I felt we could do this. The first step was to forgive each other and move past the hurt, pain and disappointment of the past.

It was time for her to come out so I spoke with Rob about taking a few days off to help her settle in. Naturally he was ok with it and as a matter of fact asked if I need any money to help out while I was off. Did I need money?! Of course. I wanted to show her everything Seattle had to offer — like Pike Place Market and the Space Needle and on and on. There were so many things to see and do. I thanked him for his generosity and support and began preparing for her arrival.

Finally she's here. I went to get her from the airport and I'm so excited to see my kid. I searched the airport for them. I found her but where was the kid? I immediately asked where's my son? She told me that she thought about it and because of the situation she thought it was best to leave him behind. My heart was broken. The joy I felt quickly turned to anger. I went through the motions for a couple of days but after that I wanted her gone. Maybe I just wanted the kid after all.

I tried to deal with her. I thought maybe spending some time together would be just the thing we needed. After all we did love each other at one time. It was no use. In my mind having the kid here gave us a shot at being a family. To me her not bringing him here meant she really wasn't giving us a shot. She didn't give us a chance in my eyes. Maybe I was wrong but this is how I felt. I decided she had to go and I made her leave. I went back to my life as Jamie Johnson. The name Herbert, the name of my grandfather and father was cursed. I didn't want anything to do with that name or anything attached to it — including my wife. Maybe it's best I go through this war by myself. After all if I go to prison I go alone. In the meantime I'm liking my life as Jamie — the person I have become. This was one of the hardest things I have ever gone through but here I am Jamie Johnson.

Jamie didn't have a past. He didn't have a mother or father. Where would he come from? Where was he born? These were some of the questions I had to ask myself. Would it be fair to fall in love with someone? If I did do I tell them everything or do I just lie and move on if I get involved in a situation that feels like love? So many questions — not many answers. I decided to stay to myself and forget. How do you forget who you are and where you come from? I would find that it's not easy to do. I had made a mess of my life and the only thing holding me down at this point was knowing that my mom and dad still loved me. I also knew that even though I didn't go to church or anything like that, God played a part in this somehow. I knew that I hadn't done what was right but I also knew that most of the people

I read about in the Bible had screwed up a time or two and God still worked things out for them I guess what I'm saying is I hope that somehow this can all work.

Chapter 9

That Little Church
(and those women)

One day at work while I'm on my grind selling shampoos and waxes, etc. out of nowhere it seems these women appeared. I didn't see them pull up and before I knew it one of them was handing me a piece of paper, a little card telling me that God said for her to tell me to come to their church. It all happened so fast I was speechless for a moment. It seemed as though she was speaking to someone or something inside of me. I was powerless against this feeling I was having and I couldn't explain it. My spirit was in agreement with hers and before I knew it I agreed to come to church as she was asking me where she could pick me up. I told here where I was living and they left just as they came. Afterwards I didn't give it much thought at all.

After work one Wednesday night I picked up some beer and showered and just as I am beginning to relax there was a knock at the door. It's the woman I met at the carwash. Well I told her I would go and I didn't see anything wrong with going to church and it wasn't like I had a whole lot going on anyway. Besides this would give me a chance to meet other people. When I arrived at the church it wasn't what I knew to be a typical church. See as a child I went to a Baptist church and this church was most definitely not Baptist. The people here were what we called, "Holy Rollers" as children. There was a church like this back home at the corner of Ave B and 12th St., as kids we would laugh when we would pass by because it was different from what we knew but even then I was curious as to what actually went on inside.

In this church I would experience some life changing events. First of all the Pastor and Elder cared about what was going on in my life. I saw and experienced things I had never seen before. I saw them lay hands on people. I never seen this before but it was real and they laid hands on me. I felt as though I didn't deserve it though. I told myself I wasn't worthy of such a thing but when I looked around in this church I could see something in the eyes of these people that I had never seen before. I desperately needed whatever it was in my life but I couldn't get passed my past. I kept thinking with those thirty (30) years hanging over my head how could I expect God to do anything for me. Look at the mess I've made of my life.

As I was thinking about my own situation I was watching what was going on in the church. The pastor was laying hands on people and they would fall back like in a trance. I didn't understand this and it didn't make sense but still I wanted it. Whatever it was I could not wait until she got to me. I wanted to fall back in this trance like state so bad but when she got to me nothing happened. I was so disappointed I felt nothing. Maybe God was angry with me and rightly so. I was the one who had gotten lost and confused in my life and turned to everything wrong but still I don't want to give up on changing, I can't give up. I made up my mind that my past wasn't going to stop me and that every time the church door opened I would be there. I must admit I didn't know what I was looking for nor did I understand what I was looking for. I didn't understand the falling back or what caused it and for the life of me I couldn't understand why I wanted it.

I kept going to church and every time they asked someone to step forward for the laying on of the hands I went. Still nothing happened. I felt nothing different inside of me. I know in my heart I wasn't playing around with this but still nothing happened until...

One night the pastor just stood me in front of the congregation and began prophesying over me. It was unlike anything I had ever encountered. Even when Mrs. Morgan came to the jail in Port Allen and said that I had the spirit of Joseph it wasn't like this. What was happening to me now was mind blowing. It actually scared me. This lady knew nothing about my past but yet she said I was running from something. She told me it was taken care of and not to be afraid. She continued to speak over me but as soon as she said those words, "It's taken care of, don't be afraid," I fell into the trance like state. I couldn't hear anything else she said. How could she have known that I was running? This had to come from above. I remember what the prophetess said months before, "If you read these Psalms, you will walk out of here." Well maybe it wasn't the way some may have wanted to walk but for me it was better than what I was facing. Because of what the previous prophetess said I had every reason to believe what the pastor was prophesying in my life right now. The question is, am I willing to receive what she is speaking over my life right now? This would be something I would wrestle with in the days and nights to come.

My pastor didn't force me to deal with my past. She and the elder just loved me for who I was. It broke my heart that I had put myself in this situation and I felt like most of the time I didn't' deserve their love or the love of God but I kept coming to church. The only time I had peace was when I was at the church. Quickly the church became my family.

Things were happening so fast in my life (p.82) I'm used to a fast paced lifestyle though. In a matter of weeks my wife had come and gone I started going to church on the regular and to make things more confusing I was intrigued by what people were saying about Phyllis' youngest daughter Julie. Phyllis has three (3) daughters and most of the time the married one drops her off at work. Well one day while I was off the youngest girl Julie brought her to work. Everyone is talking about her saying how beautiful she was and so on. I tried to act as though I didn't care but I was really very curious. I mean the other two girls aren't all that good looking and to top that off the one who usually drops her off seems to look down on us. So it seemed to me that she should be like her sisters but I still wanted to see what all the hype was about.

One morning Phyllis pulls up as usual and to my surprise everything everyone said about this daughter is true. I spoke to her in a way to let her know she was the shit but that was the extent of it as far as I was concerned. I had too much going on in my head and besides I had nothing to offer her. I mean this chick was a ten. She was clearly out of my league but I didn't see anything wrong with asking about her. I asked Rob what he knew but he didn't know much or didn't want to say anything good or bad about her. So I thought, who's better than her mom to tell me what I wanted to know BUT I had to do it on the slick. I didn't want Phyllis to suspect anything. I approached her by complimenting her on her daughters and just as any proud parent would do she began talking about her girls. I had to listen to her blab about the oldest two first but finally the conversation turned to the younger one. I couldn't help but notice she was a little guarded when speaking about Julie. She was proud of Julie's success as a realtor but she never really spoke about Julie's personal life. When it came to the oldest two she talked about one's marriage and the other's poor choices in men, but she didn't say a word about Julie having a guy in her life or friends or anything. Oh well, I was out of her league anyway so it didn't matter, however Julie was dropping her mom off more and more. The more I saw her the more curious I was about her.

Usually Julie dropped her mom off and left but this day was different. Julie pulled up to get her car washed. I had no reason to think she wanted anything more than a car wash until I noticed she was focused on me. I mean really focused. I didn't know what to think. One thing I did know was that her mom didn't like race mixing. They were German and she made it clear she was a proud German. Just from hearing her talk about current events and history etc. I knew that the East German's didn't care for Jews, or Blacks or really anyone other than themselves it seemed. It didn't bother me though because I believe that a person has the right to think or feel whatever they choose but based on the way her daughter is checking me out this might be an issue. I mean don't get it twisted I didn't have a lot but I stayed well groomed and all but would that be enough for someone like her? That was my dilemma not her mom and her issues. As for now she is just getting a car wash and maybe I'm wrong about her interest in me but something tells me I'm not.

The next time she dropped her mom off she pulled up close to where I was standing and gave me the eye. I'm thinking what does she want (really)? Maybe she hadn't seen me around and was just wondering who I was. I was a little different from most of these cats. But still I wondered, what does she want? She said hello gave me a smile and asked me my name. I spoke and told her my name and smiled back. I didn't give it much thought. I was really trying not to show too much of my curiosity towards her.

I couldn't get passed my past and not only that but what the pastor said was still burning inside of me along with what the Prophetess in Port Allen told me. I had every reason to believe these women and the church was the direction for me but the thought of being with this girl was very appealing to me. In order for me to be with her — really be with her I needed to be myself. Every time I thought of being with someone — not just her but anyone my past would replay in my mind and remind me of who I really was. I needed some answers. My life was all fucked up.

I continued to think about my life. This isn't like running from the Judge in L.A. on that ninety (90) day charge. I knew I would come out of that situation. This is different. This situation was an open and shut case. I was caught in the very act of bagging up cocaine to sell. There was no defense to that. The only hope I had started with the prophetess in Port Allen and then being lead to the church here. I'm now convinced that my focus must be on the church. I have to put all my heart and soul into it.

For the most part I had peace in this storm. The more I went to church the more hope I had. I knew that the charges would not go away and that I would have to deal with them sooner or later. Somehow I felt if I stayed away the charges would disappear. Being involved in this church had given me some hope. I wanted to be closer to God. Maybe He can make this all go away. I would still go forward to have hands laid on me and still nothing happened. I thought about faking it but I knew I couldn't fool the pastor or God so instead I prayed that I would receive whatever it was that made the people fall backwards and have this peace. The pastor would be baptizing soon. Maybe if I got baptized I would receive it then. I didn't want to be in church if it wasn't real. I didn't want to be a fake believer.

I didn't know why I couldn't receive the Holy Spirit. Maybe it was because of this one girl at church I found attractive I tried my best not to look at her in a lustful way. In spite of all the flirting Julie was doing I stayed my distance from her as well. I just didn't know why I hadn't received it yet. I stayed under the watchful eye of my pastor and I looked forward to being baptized. The thought of my past still fucked with me. It made it hard to focus but I gave it everything I had. I had lots of good days and before I knew it the time for my baptism was here.

I was nervous and excited about being baptized but afterwards I didn't feel any different and I was so disappointed. I couldn't understand it. I'm in church all the time, the pastor and the church had opened up to me but still I didn't run around and shout like they did. I didn't fall backwards. These are the things I expected I would do after being baptized but it didn't happen. Maybe it's those occasional beers. I just couldn't understand it. Why didn't I receive the Holy Ghost? My past? The beer? I just felt unworthy and so confused. In spite of these feelings I stayed in church and continued to read the Bible. I felt like it was all I had to live for.

Deep down inside there was an element of some kind pulling me away from the truth? It was telling me look at what you did. Do you really think that God would accept you like this? And at the same time the pastor is talking about hope and a future. I wanted to believe the pastor. I mean every time I picked up a Bible in prison I wasn't disappointed. It seemed as though there was a war going on inside of me and I had no control over it. Well at least I got baptized. I had been baptized before as a boy back in Sunrise, LA. I knew nothing about it then and I still know nothing about it now. I just knew I wanted it to change me.

A few days later after the church service, the pastor and one of the elders wanted to talk to me. In my way of thinking when someone says something like that it usually means bad news. I braced myself for the talk. I'm thinking what I could've done wrong. I knew I lusted after this girl once or twice but I really pretty much kept to myself. Maybe someone had noticed me looking at the girl. I just couldn't figure it out.

After pretty much everyone left the church pastor said to me, "I know you are wondering why I want to talk to you." Of course, it was killing me. She asked me, "Would you like to have an apartment?" She was talking about an apartment that was above the church. It would be available to me free of charge. She went on to say they talked about me a lot; they thought I was a good man and they didn't care about my past. It was overwhelming to know that the church cared so much about me. I was someone they barely knew. This touched my heart. This kind of love was more than I could bear. I wasn't worthy to be blessed with that apartment. First of all I couldn't forgive myself for what I have done to my family and myself. Secondly, I am running from the law. Lastly I wasn't honest with those wonderful people. My mind started racing. I can't go on like this. If I am going to stay in church I have to come clean about everything. There was no way I was going to do that now. I slowly began to turn away from the church and I began to retreat back into my shell.

Chapter 10

Julie

Just so happen Julie asked me to dinner and a movie. Her timing was perfect. I didn't want to disappoint my new found family (the church) so as I have often done in the past I ran away. It seems I ran into the direction of a waiting Julie.

Julie was nothing like what the guys and myself thought. She was kind and easy to talk to. I found that to be ideal for me. I didn't want to talk about my past and she didn't ask so I didn't volunteer any information. That one date turned into a friendship. I wasn't about to rush into anything at this time. I figured she was already involve with someone anyway I was just a distraction.

I went into the friendship with my eyes wide open. She was just too damn fine to be by herself. I had nothing to lose but everything to gain so whatever I got from Julie was all good. I felt like I couldn't lose. My past wouldn't let me get too involved with anyone so I had learned to suppress my feelings. As time went on suppressing my feelings was getting harder and harder. The more I went out with Julie the more I wanted to know her and the more I wanted her to know me. While I was building a relationship with Julie, my co- workers but my pastor wouldn't let me walk away from the church.

This wasn't at all what I expected. I was just looking for a place to live and hide from my past but here I am with friends, dating one of the baddest chicks in the city. Go figure. I was confused. All of this had a profound effect on me. You see there was a storm inside of me. It held me still. I couldn't go back but yet I couldn't go forward.

The church was good for me I knew that but I felt guilty because I hadn't been honest about my past. It didn't make sense to be with Julie either. I'm so so confused. Many times I tried to stay away from Julie, but just like the pastor at the church Julie came calling. Unlike my resistance to the pastor, I couldn't or wouldn't resist Julie.

Before long I could no longer fight my desire to be with Julie. In the beginning we would go to the homes she was selling and find ourselves making love on the floor. It was just that way with us. Go to dinner then go have sex. That suited me just fine because I didn't want or need an emotional connection to anything or anyone. It was obvious that she felt the same. At first neither of us asked the other about our pasts. It was as if we were both hiding something. As the relationship changed from friends to lovers it became very clear that there was no way to make love to someone on a consistent basis and not have any type of connection and feelings.

Our feelings for one another became very real. Julie began to open up about her past. Also, Phyllis found out about us and felt that I had betrayed her in some way. I never understood her reason for being pissed with me about Julie. We never talked about Julie and she never told me her daughter were off limits but none the less she was pissed. It made the situation at work very uncomfortable and it had to be hard on Rob. He was stuck between his best service writer and his full time cashier. Both good employees — what was he to do?

I really never wanted Phyllis to know that I was seeing Julie. I don't really know how she found out. All I know one day her sisters came to the job and blamed me for putting a rift between Julie and their mom. I didn't know it had come to this and I didn't know what to say. I knew Phyllis had her feelings about race mixing and all but we were just friends. Just dating I thought. Just dinner and sex.

One day Phyllis came in yelling at me about the kids. "Mixed kids have it harder than black kids," she said. But what the hell was she talking about. Ain't no kids. I tried to tell her Julie and I were just dating. But to Phyllis and Julie's sisters it was more. Phyllis and I started having disagreements every day at work and it had to stop. When I talked to Julie about what was going on at work, she seemed not to care. I had to care. I didn't want to hurt Phyllis. I didn't want to cause problems in their family but at the same time I wasn't willing to give Julie up. I needed answers from Julie about what was happening with her and her mother.

Julie wasn't in any kind of hurry to explain what was going on between her and her mother. Honestly, when we were together I didn't think about it either. I just didn't see what the big deal was. If Phyllis and I didn't work together I don't think I would give it much thought at all, but the fact is we did work together. Things got to the point where she couldn't come to work if I was there but it still didn't bother Julie. What Julie didn't realize was that it all fell on me. I had to face Phyllis and her two sisters. This relationship was making my work life hard.

One night at dinner Julie decided to talk about what was going on with her family and the reason they were against our relationship. It seems that she was involved in a relationship with a black guy. During the relationship there were ups and downs to say the least. Phyllis was outraged at their relationships because of her beliefs and to make matters worse he fucked over Julie. He was unfaithful and he didn't treat her as he should've. Julie continued in the relationship thinking things would get better. This put a wedge between her and her family.

Now it all made sense. She was using me to get over this guy. I was at the right place at the right time. Her heart was still with this guy. This is the reason why we never talked about anything that mattered like our past relationships or friends. It was always cut and dry. Dinner and sex. This was fine by me. As far as I was concerned I wanted it to remain this way especially after she shared her pain and disappointment in this guy with me.

I thought maybe she'll end it between us but instead it seemed we became closer. She became more open. After we talked I didn't feel sorry for her mother anymore. I felt like it was Julie's life and her decision and they should stay out of it. As long as I didn't get involved with what was going on between her and the guy, I was cool with just seeing her when she wanted to see me. I continued to suppress my feelings. In spite of my unwillingness to feel for her or tell her if I felt anything at all it seemed she wanted to see me more than ever. I was more than willing to be with her whenever she called.

There were never words like I want you in my life or anything said about being together outside of the bedroom. It was very strange to me. There was so much passion between us in the bed. The sex was crazy and yet when it was over she would get up and go. It didn't seem normal or even the way I wanted it to be.

Due to my situation and my state of mind, I just went with the flow. The more Julie and I were together it seemed the more the pastor and one of the elders knew I needed to be in church. They wouldn't give up on me. They would come to the hotel and the car wash to look for me but we would somehow always miss each other. Now I'm thinking I'm not only guilty of my past but now I have added this situation with Julie to the equation and let's not talk about how my involvement with Julie is affecting Phyllis. What was I doing to myself? What was I doing to Julie? What about Phyllis and her family?

I wanted to go back to church but I just couldn't get out of my own way. I'm not only running from the law but I am also running from myself. In the midst of all of this I must somehow try to live a somewhat normal life. Well other than the rift with Phyllis I seemed to be doing ok. The sales at the carwash were at an all-time high. I was proud to be a part of what was happening at the car wash. This made Rob happy, also he was able to tune out or should I say overlook the issues between me and Phyllis. But everything wasn't all good because Phyllis was hardly coming to work and it was because of me. I tried to tell her that Julie and I were just friends. What she needed me to say was that I wasn't sleeping with her daughter and I couldn't say that. I couldn't say what she wanted to hear. I was selfish. I wanted what I wanted.

It's time to think about things other than Phyllis and Julie. I used the baseball tickets Rob gave us for being top sellers as a way to have something else to do. A much needed distractions. Darren and Jodi would tag along sometimes. It was good to have the company and it was good to go alone. The games took my mind off of my problems for a while. What they couldn't take away was the burden of looking over my shoulder constantly.

I wanted it to end. I just didn't know how to make it end. Not having anyone to talk to about the situation didn't make it any easier. It was so much pain and to be all alone to deal with it all. I turned back to drinking again but with some control. I began to branch out and meet new people. I was saving my money. I felt like I was doing the right things and I was coming to terms with what I had done back in Port Allen.

I convinced myself that I was going to get caught one day, so I needed to enjoy the little time I had left. besides I couldn't help what would happen, next week, next month or next year. Maybe I could be out here one or two more years. Who knows? What I do know is I can't keep living looking over my shoulder.

My focus changed. I started buying clothes. I began to pull myself together mentally. I thought that Julie would be proud of me. She had been there for me. She footed the bill for everything we did together. She asked me no questions. I felt like I needed to get a better job.

There was a recycle center behind the car wash. I met some of the guys who worked there. It seemed like the kind of place I would want to be a part of but working there meant a real job and a real job meant using my real name. Am I ready for that? I had to think about this move long and hard. Becoming who I really am would increase my chances of getting caught. For my job at the carwash I didn't need to be Herbert Lawson, III. As Jamie Johnson I was doing ok. Well I lived on the edge for most of my life and I felt it was a gamble living either way. After toying with the idea for a few days I decided to go for the other job even if it meant going back to being Herbert Lawson, III. Seattle is a beautiful city full of opportunities. Am I just gonna sit around and allow this big ass monkey on my back to control me and have these pity parties every day or am I going to live? I wasn't ready to reveal my past to the church, to Julie or the car wash, but I was ready to live again on a somewhat limited basis. I decided that I wanted some kind of life in this situation.

In the meantime, I kept my thoughts to myself. It would be just a matter of time before I make my move. While I was planning my next move I did my homework. I asked the guys at the recycling center questions about what they did and who to talk to about a job. Out of respect I kept my plans and my dealing with the guys at the recycling center away from Rob and the guys at the carwash. In spite of the situation and the weight of my past and present situation I still felt that something positive could come of all of this.

I did a lot of soul searching. I didn't make a lot of money at the car wash but there was a peace there. Nobody cared anything about my past. It felt as though we all had something we were running from. It felt as though we were all equal there but it was time for a change. I needed to live — to really live. For this reason, I didn't have a problem leaving it all behind. I had given it my all.

As I learned and observed things at the recycling center I knew that things would be different. From what I could tell the people looked at you differently there. People invited you over to dinner and out to sporting events — Normal things people do when they work together and I could really get used to that. Making this change meant no more Jamie Johnson. This worked for me. Being Jamie Johnson and working at the car wash was beginning to feel like prison. I felt as though I was always trapped inside of myself. As far as I was concerned this was the worst kind of prison. This would be the change I needed. I began to prepare myself for a job at the recycling center.

Every chance I got I went over to the office and talked to the guy in the office there. I had made up my mind that a job there was mine and I wasn't taking no for an answer. Over time I had come to know the guy who did the hiring. His name was Dick. The more he said wait, the more I continued to come over to ask about getting a job there. I was so determined to work there I even went out and bought some work boots without even a sign of having the job.

Chapter 11

New Job...Old Life

I just wasn't going to be denied. Now I just need to come up with a plan. I decided to just go in for work one day. When I got there I just followed the guys in. I couldn't go in and see dick because he would know that I hadn't been hired. The plan was to go inside the recycling center and tell the guy Bruce who managed the warehouse that I was a new hire.

As I go in the warehouse I see this assembly line with niggas lined up on both sides. As I stood there some guy said, "You must be new. Go to Bruce's office and tell him Dick said put you to work." As I am walking to Bruce's office I hear this loud voice over the machines. It's Bruce. I shake his hand and tell him exactly what the guy told me to say. That worked out fine, but I still had to fill out the application so I decided that if it worked once it could work again. This time I went to Dick and told him that Bruce said I needed to fill out an application.

Thank God it worked! Today is the beginning of a new place in my life. Jamie Johnson had served me well but I wanted

my name back. I knew that my name meant a whole lot
of trouble but Hebert Lawson, III is who I am. I wanted
to still have my family at the car wash but Jamie Johnson
was who they knew and loved. The crew at the recycling
center would know Herbert. The two places were too close
together for this to work so the best thing to do was to cut
ties at the car wash. Damn! What about Julie? I wasn't ready
to tell her about Herbert and I wasn't ready to give her up
either. I was looking forward to telling her about the job but
first I have to tell Rob something. I was making that place
a lot of money and my leaving would be a big blow to Rob.
The more I made he made.

After my first day of work at the center I walked over
to the carwash and told Rob about my new job. He was
disappointed to lose me but he was also happy for me. I
owed so much to Rob for giving me a chance to make it in a
place where I knew nothing about anything or anybody. He
gave me something to build on and I will always be grateful.
I wanted him to know that but now it's back to being
Herbert and I must leave the car wash behind. In making
this decision I had to be very careful not to see anyone from
the car wash. It would just be too confusing for them to call
me Jamie and my new coworkers who know me as Herbert.

A new door has opened and I had no idea what life was going to be like working at the recycling center. It felt right just like the car wash did but it was slightly different. My past didn't seem to be my every thought now and that was a relief. Before getting this job for days and weeks all I thought about was my past. Now I am determined not to live locked up inside of my own mind. Well I told Rob, also I decided it was time to tell Julie. I could just imagine how proud she would be but it had to wait a few days. It seemed like she was busy at work and with my new job I got caught up in the moment so it ended up being about a week before I saw her. She finally called and asked me to dinner as she often did. I could hardly get through the day thinking about how happy she would be for me.

And to my surprise it wasn't that way. She acted as though I had done something wrong. I spent a few minutes wondering what did I say or maybe it's the old boyfriend. I really had no clue as to why she reacted this way. The smart thing to do was not to push her even though I really wanted to know what made her sad. After dinner we went back to my hotel room and made love. The lovemaking was the same — full of passion everything was there, but deep down I knew something was different.

Even after her reaction to my new job, I kept my focus. The whole time I was working on getting this job my thought was she didn't have to pay for dinner all the time anymore. I could get out of this hotel and get a place I could bring her to and feel good about it; a place to wine and dine her just like she did for me. Well I decided to just keep grinding at work, saving money and staying focus on living. I didn't just want to show Julie I was more than what she saw, I also wanted to do this for me. I mean who knows when my freedom would end? Eventually my past would catch up to me and when the day comes I wanted to be able to say, "I tried to do right." There are people who can vouch for that fact and this would be part of my defense. I really believed that would work.

As the days went on I was getting closer to my new co-workers and the car wash was quickly becoming a distant memory. That felt good until I realized I was seeing Julie less and less. At first I didn't know if it was me getting more involved with the guys at work and going out with them more or if it was her avoiding me. I really couldn't tell. I was becoming comfortable in my new environment and it felt so right. At the car wash everything was a lie. I felt like an actor in this four (4) or five (5) hour epic movie. Kinda like *Gone with the Wind*. Leaving the car wash that was one thing but Julie that was another. You just don't leave someone you made love to like they don't exist anymore. At this point it was out of my hands and I knew that something just wasn't right.

I started thinking I have to make time to see her. This is a big step for me and here it is the one person I want to share it with is no longer around. After work one day I am sitting in my hotel room and there's a knock at the door. It's her looking as beautiful as ever. Right away my doubts and fears were gone. The joy of seeing her outweighed any negative thoughts I may have had before she knocked on that door. But the look in her eyes...it wasn't the same as it was in the beginning. Still I was happy to see her, but it was obvious that she had something on her mind. It's something she came to talk about. She wanted to go have dinner. Dinner seemed like the perfect time to tell her all my heart. Before she could say a word I began to ramble on about my new job and friends I'd met and telling her about the next step for me but before I could tell her anything else she asked, "Why did you leave the carwash?" She said she thought I was happy there. She said if I needed more money she was there for me and she felt it was too soon for me to make this move. I felt I needed to make my life better and getting the job was one way of doing that.

Now it's all starting to make sense. She felt she had control as long as she had the money. She needed me to need her. That must have made her comfortable. Obviously that was the thing with the ex-boyfriend. It was clear now why she was disappointed in my decision to move on. My hope was that she would come to see things my way but I still walked away from dinner confused. Where I came from women wanted and insisted that you better yourself. I spent the next few days trying to figure out what went wrong.

I asked myself was I open enough? After some careful thinking I could not come up with anything I could have done to push her away. The only thing that I could come up with was to look at her last relationship and from what she told me the last guy had other women and he took her for granted. I think she felt she needed to have total control with the next guy. That's just not who I am and my heart went out to her. I had to move on in spite of how I felt about her. My time was short. There's so much hanging over my head and a new job and new people was what I needed.

The next step for me was to get out of that hotel and get an apartment. Don't get me wrong, I wasn't ashamed of the hotel, but I wanted better for me. In my spare time I began to look at apartments and soon after Julie and I drifted apart I met someone else. There was no physical attraction at first. She had broken up with her boyfriend and needed a place to crash.

She wasn't a bad looking chick. After talking to her I found we had a lot in common. We both talked a lot and I really enjoyed being with her plus I really needed a friend. The more I saw her the closer she got to me. I had put this wall up around me and it didn't seem to bother her at all something was telling me she knew I was running from something. We did what people in need do — we reached out to one another. At times we made love but we kept it friendly. I guess you could call it friends with benefits. I was just getting over Julie and I didn't want to be that close to anyone at least not yet. I wouldn't let this chick in at all and she seemed to understand. I liked that about her. Yes, I know that is selfish of me but that's just how I saw it and right about now I wanted more of what Seattle had to offer. I threw myself on the club scene and what I was about to experience was going to blow my mind.

I thought Seattle was the shit after experiencing the club scene. I put the Seattle club scene right up there with Los Angeles clubs I used to hang in back in the day. I think I'm going to be alright now. If I had any doubt I don't anymore.

This club I liked Hollywood Underground was all that and more to me. It was everything you could want in a club. Everybody that was somebody in and all around Seattle was coming to this club. Women of every color, shape and size was in this joint. Needless to say Julie became a distant memory. My life became my job and Hollywood Underground. I quickly began to fit right in and it wasn't long before I met someone else. I didn't want to move too fast. I was new to Seattle and I wanted to take my time. One night I was sitting at the bar having a few drinks. As always there are beautiful women all over the club but sitting next to me is this beautiful Filipino chick and every chance she got she made small talk with me.

I wasn't focused on one chick that night. There were many I could have talked to but she seemed to have her eyes on me. She was feeling good, having a few drinks and I noticed she was by herself. The more she drank, the more she talked to me. I must admit having this beautiful chick hit on me was an ego booster. I wasn't really looking for anybody that night. I was just there to dance and feel the place out. However, this girl seemed very much into me. Now I was never one to turn down an advance from a chick and I wasn't going to start now. After a few shots I turned my attention to this beautiful chick who's been hitting on me.

The first thing she says to me is, "Hey, how old do you think I am?" I'm thinking you are so pretty who gives a fuck? It must have meant a lot to her because she asked me again, "Come on, how old do you think I am?" Well she obviously looked younger than what she really was. That was a no brainer. She was proud of herself. I just took an educated guess and said something like, "About 25." She said, "No, I'm 40." I swear she didn't look no older than 25 so it blew my mind when she said she was 40. I could put her side by side with a 25 year old any day and she would be right there. This chick top to bottom was one of the finest chicks in the club and not only that she chose me, right then and there.

That night she went back to my hotel and after that night we saw each other almost every day. It was so easy to be with her. She didn't dig into my personal life and she was ok with my friend with benefits chick. She even had her own restaurant and brought me dinner almost every night. I was very impressed but I wanted more. The more I went to the clubs the more women I wanted to date. Besides I thought the Filipino was moving too fast.

The whole city and club scene was new to me and although she was everything a man could want I didn't want to be tied down right now. I just wasn't ready for her in that way. I wanted to stay focused. I didn't want to bring someone into my screwed up world. My life and all of its secrets were just too much to put on someone you could love. Think about it running from thirty (30) years, always looking over my shoulder, that's crazy shit. It's just not right to burden this chick or any other chick down with that kind of shit.

I began to pull away as she got closer. Looking in her eyes I had no reason to pull away, but it was the only thing I knew to do to keep us from getting closer. I knew my pulling away would hurt her, but in my mind it was the only way. She had lots of questions and I just couldn't tell her the truth. I knew she was good for me but my past would win this battle as well. It always had a way of getting the best of me.

After blowing my chances with two beautiful women and the constant looking over my shoulder, I couldn't deal with myself sober anymore. Just like taking a pig out of a pig pen and bringing him into the house clean him up and he's one of the family but let him out of the house he'll run right back to the pig pen he came from because he's a pig. I returned back to the old me. I became a regular at my favorite club and needless to say I would cross paths with the Filipino chick again. This time it was obvious she hated me for what I had done. She had every right. She felt I had no reason to let her go and I understood that. She didn't know why I did what I did and I couldn't explain it to her. I guess that hurt the most. If I could have explained it to her I think she would have understood. I didn't have the guts to be real with her, so I just moved on. I did what I wanted and if I got lonely, my friend with benefits was still around when I needed her. It seemed she would always be there when I needed her.

Maybe she had hopes of us being together. Maybe we would've been good together. She asked nothing of me and did everything I asked of her. I recall one night I went out clubbing with one of the guys from work. I left her in the room and she said she would be waiting when I came back. Well the guy and I got shit faced. When we finally settled on a club I saw this white chick sitting at the table with these guys. For some reason she caught my eye and I just had to say something to her. Maybe it was the alcohol. Nevertheless at the risk of stepping on somebody's toes I went out on a limb and had a few words with her. To my surprise the niggas she was sitting with was cool and it didn't seem to bother them. She was kind considering the situation I had put her in. In my drunken state I went too far.

I should have just admired her from my seat and that was my intention but I had too many drinks and took it to another level. I insisted on her dancing with me and so on and so on. At some point started disrespecting her as a woman by calling her out of her name. The next thing i knew I was having words with the niggas at the table and then swinging at this dude. After that, all I remember is getting my ass kicked. By the time it was over I was sober and bloody. I do remember during the ass kicking looking for Tubby Cain the cat I came with. I looked up and he had this 20 foot long pole. I said to myself what the fuck is he going to do with that? Now this was at the end of the fight. I don't know where he was at the beginning. I didn't know him very well and he must have felt the same way. He was probably somewhere saying, "I'm not going to get the shit beat out of me for this nigga I hardly know. " I just said fuck it and somehow I managed to get back to the hotel with Cain's help. I had no broken bones but I was sore as hell with a chipped tooth and a well -whooped ass. My girl was there. She took care of me for the next few days since I could not go to work. First of all I was somewhat ashamed and second I was too sore to get out of bed. This was just an example of the kinds of things this chick did for me. She didn't have a lot, but what she had she was willing to give to me — her time, her kindness, whatever. Still she wasn't the one I wanted.

Though I was limited in where I went, I fell in love with
Seattle and even after getting my ass kicked I still came away
feeling like this city and I were made for each other. I wanted
to be here in spite of my situation. I knew I was limited but I
wanted to be myself again. I don't remember at what point I
had come to the decision to just be me, past and all.

Maybe I was just tired of all the worrying about the past. It
had finally become too much to bear and I just wanted to
live again a somewhat normal life. I needed to understand
that I would get caught and come to terms with that truth
and I did. That's when I began to enjoy Seattle and all
that it had to offer. For me that was back to all the things
that led me to this dark place in my life. I went on a ride
I would never forget. I would come to know people of all
races. Not only that I would become friends with a couple
of Seattle Supersonics' star players. That alone opened up
a whole new and different kind of world and woman to me.
I guess you could say I was part of the groupie scene. I was
surrounded by all of these groupie bitches and this was
something different and I loved it. Most of the girls saw me
as a go between. They felt if they could get close to me they
could get close to the players.

Chapter 12

Hollywood Underground and the NBA

Believe you me I played the go between role for everything it was worth. Two of the players X-McDaniel and Olden was loving every minute of it as well. The team was winning and these two players had good numbers. These cats were the core of the team and because of my friendship with them I was right in the middle. Hollywood Underground was responsible for me meeting them and all the bitches that came along with them. This was the highlight of coming to Seattle. Julie was behind me. But leaving the Filipino chick alone was a hard pill to swallow because I felt so much guilt but I just wanted to experience so much more.

My job is going good, the club scene is jumping and I'm finally ready to get an apartment. I found a nice crib near downtown on the 7th floor. I got a view of the skyline and it's incredible. Growing up in San Francisco I knew what a view should look like because San Francisco had it all. With that being said Seattle is a beautiful city and I felt blessed to be here.

Back at work friendships were being made and I was having so much fun with the guys. Friends who wasn't dealing dope was such a change for me and a much needed one. They were regular people. And for such a long time these kind of people had been missing from my life. Just so happen the same guy who had taken me out clubbing, the night I got my ass kicked, became my closest friend on the job. We were all close but Tubby Cain made it clear he wanted to hang out with me and I welcomed his friendship a little more than the others.

This guy invited me to his house and I became friends with his wife and kid. We just clicked in spite of his ass coming up missing the night of the fight. There were others on the job I had gotten to know, guys like Larry, William, and Rickey, who was the lead man on the job. Rickey was going through a transformation at this time. He was going from drinking and drugs to staying sober and clean. I guess he saw something in me that reminded him of what he was going through.

the guys at work knew I was one who worked hard on the job but partied hard after hours. My activities after work included drinking and drugs. I think Rickey didn't want me to go through what he had been through. Little did he know I had been where he had been twice if not more. Still knowing that he cared meant a lot to me. I guess I just wanted to fit in. Then again, my past always played a big part in my behavior. While I was drinking my past didn't exist so it seemed. I was able to convince myself that everything was normal and I wanted my co-workers to think it really was. As long as I acted normal there was no reason for anyone to think otherwise. At least that was my theory and for the most part it worked. So far I had managed to cover up the past and now I'm excited about the future. I loved my apartment and I was meeting lots of women, most of them one night stands.

Speaking of one night stands, there was a parade of some kind. People were everywhere. I was drunk and having a ball. Somehow I ran into this beautiful ass chick and we just started talking and walking together. Before I knew it after walking for what seemed like hours we were at her crib. I'm sober by now and I'm looking at this bad ass chick and said to myself, "What the fuck am I doing here?" The crib was on a hill in a nice neighborhood. This chick had it all so it seemed and here she is out at a parade picking up guys. That thought only lasted for a moment. I was just glad it was me and it was no talking about it she wanted to have sex. Right after we did she made it clear that she was never going to see me again. What had just happened meant nothing to her and I was told not to get her number off the phone. Well that's exactly what I was thinking of doing and that's what I tried to do. She caught me and kicked me out. Oh well, I was totally please with the way the night went down.

If I wasn't at the clubs or having these one night stands, I was spending a lot of time alone. When I was alone I reflected on how I had fucked up my life. If only it was different, if only I didn't have the drug charge in Port Allen. What if?! It seems what if had become a part of my life. Thank God for Tubby Cain and his invitations to hang out at his house on the weekends. It helped to take my mind off all the bullshit that was going on in my head. We were so much alike, man.

We enjoyed drinking of course and cooking. We had the same taste in music. It was great. Cain liked going to the clubs in the hood and me I was into the upscale joints. That was ok though because clubbing in different places gave us something to talk about on Mondays when we returned to work. No matter what happened at Hollywood Underground Cain never wanted to come and it was the same with me at the hole in the walls he liked.

There was something I couldn't help but notice about Cain's life. His girlfriend had a real distrust for him. You could hear it in her voice. And rightfully so, Cain was very unfaithful to her and just like millions of other women in the world she stayed around hoping that maybe, just maybe things would get better. Nine times out of ten it doesn't. Other than that they were fun to be around and I tried to see her side of it. However, Cain had embraced me as a friend and I felt as a man my loyalty was to him. After all I was no different from Cain. How could I throw stones at him? Hell I'm living in a glass house. There was one thing I didn't and wouldn't do and that was encourage him in that behavior. After getting to know her I felt she deserved his faithfulness but I just kept that thought to myself for the time being. Hell, I was still in the club observing the ladies not really ready to settle myself. I lived in a glass house too.

Yes! I wanted someone, yet my past haunts me and I'm telling myself I just can't bring someone into this lie. But as always there's a side of me that lives on the edge and this side of me somehow wins out and risks whatever's on the line. And this has been something I've come to know about myself and often I've fought it, but to no avail. I've never been able to overcome this desire to live this way. And at the club there's all kinds of ladies and I was keeping my distance. But for some reason the bartender caught my eye. A beautiful chick inside and out. And it was clear to me we had some kind of attraction to each other and I found myself spending most of the night talking to her and still I wasn't ready to commit at least not now, but there were these twins, one I was crazy about, they was groupie bitches and you know what's funny, I didn't care. Because I had gotten to know them and one of them I'll call Susan was more my speed a little over the top.

A risk taker, man! She just blew me away. And she knew I hung out with X and Olden, I knew that's why she and others wanted to know me and for some reason I didn't mind that either. And over time she and I would go at each other, well! On my part it was jealousy and for her I think she just like fucking with me knowing I was crazy about her. Matter of fact, I even found myself getting ball players for this girl. Knowing how it made me feel. But I would do almost anything for this chick. And it had gotten to the point that when some of the players would come to Seattle to play they would come to the club and look for me to get them bitches. Man! Groupie bitches are a different breed, most of the time, all it took was me saying (see my nigga over there looking this way), he play for the Knicks or whoever the team maybe and the chick would be gone to this cat before I could finish talking.

Those niggas must have gotten together and spread the word about me getting them bitches, because no matter what team came to town I was the one who would hook them up with chicks. Needless to say in spite of my feelings for baby girl, I played it for everything it was worth. I really enjoyed hanging out with the players; I've met so many I can't even name all of them. And because of X and Olden I sat court side at times. I felt part of the team, so to speak. And the thing I enjoyed the most was the times in the club with X and Olden chicks would come up to us asking those guys questions and other bullshit. And eventually my name would come up, like who are you, do you play. And X would say shit like, that's Herb he play, c'mon you never seen him? He ride the bench and I'm wanting to laugh, but I'm trying to play along to see where this goes and it was times when chicks would ask for my autograph.

Times like that was funny, and I enjoyed every minute of it! (To be honest) I have no answer for why those guys like me, all I know I was real and I didn't want anything from them, well! I can't say that because I did get all the tickets I wanted and even in the club I got all the drinks I could drink ok! Let's go back to the bartender, not only was she working in the club, she also worked at Boeing. Man! This girl had everything I could want in a woman. She owned a home just outside the city and when I wasn't running around the club chasing bitches, I knew she was the one, but just the thought of that twin being my girl made me hold off on everybody else. You see! When the Sonic's was on the road, I saw moments of the real person when we talked, and it seemed I could tell her that what she's doing isn't cool. And I seemed to get her attention for a little while and before the nights over

She would ask me about some basketball player, she had saw me talk to. And I knew the bartender chick saw me go through all this shit with these groupie bitches. And I just figured she didn't want to have anything to do with me. But she didn't seem to mind any of that craziness that came with me. She wanted me and that was it. But I knew I wouldn't be faithful and she didn't deserve to be hurt because that's what I do, I hurt the ones who love me, somehow I tried to keep my distance from her, because I just refuse to hurt her. Besides I was very happy with the one-night stands. But truly on the inside I wanted love, but I didn't want to open up. Because I knew that the one I'm with at that awful time, will have to endure the pain of being caught up in a standoff with the law, and not only that being separated from one another not knowing if we'll ever see each other again. Besides I knew what that the D. A. had offered me so falling in love with someone and leaving them to this bullshit. I didn't want that!

Now can you see why I was confused, also I've found this place in my life where I want to stay (Seattle)? And only if I can turn back the hands of time, but that's not reality and I got to face real life. Nevertheless the more I'm here in this city, the harder it is to face my past, somehow I just got to forget it and move on. And I knew one way that would help me to move on and that was to hit the club hard on weekends and I did just that. And I also got involved with my friends at work and as I said before my man! Tubby Cain kept me over at his crib, and there was Larry and Williams, and others who would be hired along the way, that would make this journey a little easier for me. But I can't fool myself and say it'll go away with time, that's just not going to happen. Needless to say deep down inside I was hoping for a girl, in spite of all the bullshit I wanted someone to come, I didn't know when or how. I just wanted it to be right, because in my heart I would know. So I just continue to work and go to the Hollywood Underground,

Mostly just to dance, man! I was sick and tired of the one night stands somewhat, because most of the bitches I ended up seeing again and that's not what a one night stand is, it's one night, but when I got drunk it's another night with this chick I meant to spend one just one night with. Man! My life on the run was one big twisted bad dream. But to me somehow it was normal and to the poor fucks that observed me, must have thought I was out of control and I was at times. But it was the best I could do. Because what I was facing was like getting a life sentence and no doubt that was hard to swallow. Nevertheless I knew I couldn't go on feeling sorry for myself, so I had fun at work and played hard on weekends. I was determined to make the best of the situation, well! I open up a bank account, also I started to do things to the apartment, like adding a plant here and there, I mean! It was already furnish so I didn't have that to deal with and besides the furniture wasn't' bad.

Hey! I was simple and the furniture was the least of my problems. Oh! I had to get some music, and of course I needed some earrings and watches, so I opened up an account at a jewelry store downtown. I have clothes, man! I'm feeling good about myself, in spite of the shit that played on my mind. Well!

Chapter 13

Yolanda, Fat Cat and the Call Girl

A beautiful thing happened to me on the way home from work. It was a normal day as always I flirted with lots of chicks downtown on my way home but this day there's this young black chick, beautiful and with a body to match. And I flirted with her as I would do with any other chick, but to my surprise she was game and gave me her phone number or maybe I gave her mine, anyway! We connected sometimes later, could've been a week, a month I don't exactly remember. And up to now besides the chick at the hotel, I had only been with white girls and that wasn't by design for some reason it just was happening that way.

But this girl was different, she was young and sweet, very quiet and everything I needed at this time. But I must confess I didn't think I had a prayer with this girl. But at first we didn't have a lot to talk about. Well! For one thing I'm this older dude who have been around the block a few times. And this chick after a few times on the phone with her I knew she wasn't like the others. She was too good for me, but being me I wanted what I wanted and I wanted her.

Well! All those old bitches in the club, who needs them, they were just one night stands anyway, man! I felt good about this chick. No it wasn't love at first sight or anything like that, but I felt renewed inside for the first time in a long time, I was finally looking forward to needing someone and to me that's what I needed. In the beginning she would just listen to me for hours on the phone. And to me that's what I liked, maybe because I can talk a lot. I had only seen her that one time downtown

And after talking to her on the phone for what had seemed like months, I felt close to her. Before Yolanda came into my life, I wasn't' calling any females on the phone and talking for hours. Nothing like that, oh! Yes I had my eye on a few but not to this extent. It was only one-night stands. Well! The only people I was close to was Cain and his family. But as far as the kind of closeness you get from a woman, the kind I was running from. But for some reason I wanted that closeness with Yolanda. Maybe it was the innocence I saw in her, whatever it was, she is the one for me. And knowing she was young, I knew it was going to take time and unlike with the others I had plenty of time for her. I didn't want to blow this one, in spite of my past and the thirty (30) years I'm facing back in Louisiana, meeting this girl, it all seemed to not matter as much. And with her in my life I wanted to go forward. I wasn't in a hurry to lay with her (that was coming), I knew that. Besides I'm still going to the club.

I was getting lots of sex, I just wanted her to take her time, I mean! I was saying all the right things. So it was no pressure. Well! In the meantime my mom called and said my cousin Fat Cat wanted to come out here. Needless to say I was a little worried about that, oh! Don't get me wrong I love my cousin, but as I understood it he was running on a drug charge and of course I was doing the same. And what really made me scared was this would just increase my chances of getting caught. And not only that I've just met the sweetest chick. But this is Fat Cat not only was he my cousin but he was the closest thing to a best friend. Man! We've been through a lot of shit together and every time I needed him, he was there for me. So it was a no brainer, I had to say yes. And as I thought about it would be good for me to have somebody here who knew me. And Fat Cat knew me better than almost anybody, he was the ideal person to have out here. We understood each other and more importantly we liked each other.

And the more I thought about it the more I liked the idea. And at work the business was growing and they were bringing in more people. So the timing was right for him to come out. And the only thing I asked of him was to leave the dope game back there. And when I talked to him about coming, I made that clear and he agreed and I was relieved that he agreed! So the next thing I needed to do was go to my boss about getting him a job when he gets here. And my boss said yes. And I told Fat Cat what I was doing to make it easier for him when he gets here. And all to do now was to just wait for him, also I was building a relationship with Yolanda, talking to her on the phone, I could tell she wasn't ready to come over to my crib just yet. I knew before she was to commit I would have to meet her mom and dad. Man. My lifestyle was so different from hers and I thought about that, how would that play out

With her family, and the question I needed to ask myself, was I willing to give up some of my bad behavior like running around with all kinds of chicks and drinking like a sailor? Man! All this shit was what I've become. Not only was I bringing baby girl into a life on the run but add bitches and drinking to it. It's insane, but I wanted what I wanted (needless to say) all my adult life, and being on the run I thought would change me (apparently not). Because I knew the way I had chosen, she was going to get hurt or I would be taken away from her. And at the beginning I wanted to be the person for her and the Lord knows that was my intention. But I was getting comfortable in my mess, forgetting about the monkey that's on my back. Don't get me wrong in a way I wanted to forget and move on, just leave the past behind me, but at the same time it wasn't' a good idea to get too relaxed in my situation. Knowing that it's thirty (30) years

I'm facing. And after many phone calls and getting to know each other. It's obvious I'm gonna have to go over to her house and meet her parents before she feels comfortable coming over to my crib and somehow I put all the bullshit aside and went over to her house and met everybody. And to my surprise it was real cool and relaxing, it was different her family was close; especially her and her mom. I knew one thing, her mom would have a lot of influence on her. And I would need to have patience and to be honest I was ready to wait and in spite of my crazy lifestyle I had love for her. And back at work everyone was looking forward to meeting my cousin Fat Cat. I had talked about him a lot since I've known he as coming for sure. And I must admit I was looking forward to his arrival as well. But just as in the past, you never know when one of our family members will show up. So knowing this I just went about my life as always.

And then one day there's a knock on the door and its Fat Cat, not only Fat Cat but also he has a woman with him. OK! I could understand a woman. Ok! She has to know he's running from the law, a very beautiful chick I might add, but that's not the end, not one kid but two. Right now! I'm thinking this nigga is crazy to have this chick and kids caught up in this crazy shit. But because of my love for (Cat) I didn't ask any questions. Mainly because I knew he would tell me what was going on (sooner or later). Besides he needs me right now and at this point the only thing that matters is we are family and we knew that came before anything else. So my only thing now is to make them as comfortable as I can. Hey! I only have a two bedroom apartment but it's gonna have to work and when they got here that day Fat Cat and myself went to the store to get some drinks. Man! I haven't seen this cat for a minute, remember now I was in Port Allen locked up and before that I was in Chino locked up so it had been a minute since I've seen this dude.

Needless to say! I didn't know this chick, and as I've always said if you love her (I like her). And until I see different that's what I go with. And after coming back from the store with the drinks it was a time of reflecting back on the times Fat Cat and I had in Port Allen, Compton and San Francisco, etc. We had been through a lot together. Also it was a time for me to get to know his girlfriend (Rony). She had two kids and the oldest was a young boy, I'll say he was about 12 years of age and he wasn't Fat Cat's kid. But the other kid, who was a little girl, not even a year old and just like all Fat Cat's kids she looked just like him. And she was from a little place northwest of New Orleans called Salt Pete, St. Rose, and Man! We must have stayed up all night just drinking and talking. Well! My first impression of Rony was she was real cool, but I noticed something right away. She wasn't like most of the chicks I'd seen him with in the past. I felt she wanted to control him and he didn't seem to mind her controlling ways. Matter of fact

If he love a girl it's nothing he wouldn't do for his girl. Well! I guess most guys are that way and now that I think about it, it wasn't that strange, but this was different, he bent over backwards a little too much for this chick I thought. But who am I to judge, besides I didn't know anything about her. All I know is she kept the drinks flowing that night and right away I could tell she was a little street and I love that about a woman. It's Friday and we got a couple of days to party and see a little of the city, my first thought was Hollywood Underground , but there's one problem, no baby sitter. So we kind of just stayed at the crib and cooked and drank all weekend. Well! After sobering up there was something I wanted to know, like what's his plan for the future and did he really want the job. And last but not least how serious are his charges. Because it was important to me that we stayed away from any dealing of drugs and so on, at least as long as he was staying with me.

Needless to say! I guess at the time he was going to say all the right things and being new to the city it would take time to find that kind of bullshit. You see! The job paid real good money and to have his family with him and not only that, being able to get a job right away was the perfect thing for him. And I was happy for him, look! He has a chance to see what I see, and if he really wants it, it could work out for them. And when he gets caught he'll have something to say about what he's been doing since running on the charge, you never know, at least that's how I see it! I thought if you can show some kind of change just maybe the D.A. and judge would consider that, you never know. Meanwhile! I'm looking forward to Monday, hey! By the way this dude didn't have to start out the way I did, on the streets and then in a shelter. I was just happy to be there for him, but I must admit I was worried about Fat Cat putting his heart into this.

I realize that it's not the kind of money he was making in the dope game, but the way I see it, you're buying time and anything could happen between now and the time you get caught. I really believed that something good could come out of this. Well! After them guys are settled in Fat Cat is working and he seems to be loving it and everybody at the job is crazy about him. And I'm glad for him and his family. And now I must get back to doing my club things. I mean! It was part of what I've come to love about the city. Besides the bartender chick , who loved getting me drunk, and also I enjoyed fucking with her head. So I was ready to get back to the club. But before I go any further - one Friday after work, I went to the bank downtown to deposit my check as I do on Friday. And when coming out of the bank a badass chick caught my eye, I mean! This wasn't nothing new, its all kinds of beautiful chicks downtown. But this was different and taking another look at this beautiful chick, and as I looked a second time to catch a glimpse at that ass.

I notice she was looking back I just knew she wasn't looking at me, but I was curious and I continue to look back at her as well and finally I said, "Fuck it," it's time to go back and say something, and as I turn around, she had did the same and was coming my way, or at least that's how I saw it, and to my surprise she approached me and asked me about a good restaurant here downtown. Oh! That wasn't what got me it's the way she said it, she had this beautiful French accent. Well! Needless to say I'm standing there looking at this beautiful French chick, first of all, I'm thinking she has to be a model or actress, and what is she doing talking to me, man! I got nothing to offer this chick. Anyway! Here downtown there's all kinds of fancy joints. So I ask her what kind of food she was interested in. I can't remember what she said, all I know is she invited me to have dinner with her, of course I wasn't dressed for dinner just getting off work. But I didn't live far from here so I asked her if she would come to my place.

And I'll shower and get dressed for dinner, and to my surprise she was cool with that. So we got a cab and went to my place, Fat Cat and Rony was home cooking dinner, etc. and I introduced her to them but I couldn't pronounce her name anyway! It sounded so good when she said it. Well! While I showered of course Rony was entertaining her. Needless to say! I was eager to see what was going to happen this night, so I got dressed and we hopped in a cab back downtown, to a restaurant. And need I say it was a beautiful thing here I am at dinner with this beautiful model chick, and guess what! It didn't cost me anything. And of course I got lots of questions and she's just sitting here looking at me, with this sexy smile (first thing I wanted to know), who are you and what are you doing here in Seattle, then I paused and she said she was a model and she was doing a T.V. commercial, and most importantly, why me. But to be honest I didn't know what to think. So I'm just going with the flow.

Waiting to see what's going to happen after dinner, and now the moment of truth, I enjoyed the dinner and of course I'm a little drunk. And to my surprise she didn't waste no time. She invited me to her hotel room, she said she was going to get into the hot tub, that was in the room, of course I said yes and we went to the hotel. I think it was the Westin hotel, and it's one of the best hotels in Seattle for sure in the top ten. I know I couldn't afford nothing like this, not only was this chick beautiful she had class also. Hey! It wasn't a whole lot to say, once we were in the room she sat in the hot tub, I didn't have time to think, man! I just followed her lead, and just got my ass into that hot tub and fast. She made me feel so comfortable as if she just wanted someone to hold her, it seemed as though she was lonely for kissing and hugging. As I said before I just followed her lead. Needless to say! It was lots of kisses and hugging. We made love in the hot tub of course and

In the bed, I mean it was crazy and after an evening of making love, I fell asleep holding her and all of a sudden a beeper goes off in the room. I wake up and look for her and then I look at the time and damn it's about 2:00 a.m. she apologized for waking me up and says she has to go, saying she didn't want me to leave, she said just stay here in bed. I have no clue to what's going on. She said it's her manager or something to that effect. Anyway! I thought it was a little strange, but I don't know how that shit works and within the hour she was back, Hey! It wasn't my business and I didn't ask about the call. Well! We talked and made love again then her beeper goes off again. And she made a call and said she has to go again. Well! This time I know something is going on with this girl. And again she asked me to stay and of course I did, and waited like a good boy until she got back, not knowing if she would

Open up to me and talk about what's going on. Besides she wasn't my girl and didn't have to explain anything to me. But I just thought I'll ask anyway, and she did come clean, but it wasn't going to change my feelings, because I didn't feel anything, it was just sex. But she wanted me to know what she did. And she said she didn't want to tell me at first because she felt it would drive me away. I said, "What is it? You can tell me, it's nothing you could be doing that would make me walk away from this night, and to be honest it really wasn't anything, and looking at her, I could tell she believed me. And there was an innocence about her, maybe that was what attracted me to her the first time I laid eyes on her. And as she got back into bed she wanted to lay it on the line. Well! She said she was a call girl, I was really surprise, yes! I've been around and I've seen a lot of shit, but I really thought she was a model, or maybe I just wanted

Her to be a model, you be the judge. And she along with others was traveling the country, to all the major cities making a lot of money. Needless to say I've always been fascinated with that lifestyle as a young man in San Francisco. And truth be told I was honored to be with her, I guess everyone wants to be chosen, and I'm no different. Well! That was just half of it, she wanted to share with me what had happened to her sometime back, I don't know how I didn't see it but it was a scar on the back of her body, up close it looked like someone threw some sort of hot liquid on her, well! The way she explained it, this cat burned her as a way of having power over her. I've been around long enough to know that one of the ways these cats control these chicks is "fear" in some cases this kind of shit, could last a lifetime. Obviously the physical scar will never go away, but more than that the mental scar seemed to be more serious.

Hey! I'm no psychic but after spending sometime downtown Los Angeles and Hollywood, you see this type of shit all the time, and truly I felt her pain, and besides I had scars of my own, the only difference was my scars was self-inflicted, (none the less) a scar is a scar, and every scar has a story. Well! By the time we got past the scars the weekend was coming to an end. And for the first time in a long time I was taken back to a place where I thought I wanted to forget, Los Angeles, a place where there were so many ups and downs for me. Who said you can't go back, Man! After her story I didn't know whether to kiss her or kill her for taking me back there. Maybe it was my destiny to meet her, just to see how far I have come and it wasn't getting any, better but what do I do with myself. I can't go back into my mother's womb and be born again, can I?

Chapter 14

Back to Reality

Well! Sunday morning is here and I must have been real tired, because she is gone and I didn't even hear her leave, no last kiss goodbye, I guess that's how it goes and as I looked around in amazement, and on the night stand it was a roll of cash. And until this day I'm still trying to figure out what the money was for. Ok! Back to reality it's Sunday and it's work tomorrow and I can't wait to see Tubby, (saying to myself) he's going to love this one. And at home, I thought what will Rony think of me, but this is the kind of shit she'll see as long as they are living with me. But still I didn't want to give her the wrong impression, so I was either going to be a player or someone who just use bitches up. Not that it would have mattered to me anyway, but I didn't know her and I didn't want her to think I was a Son of a bitch, and I was but at the end of the day I was just being me.

Also there was something happening inside of me, you see the fear of being caught was finally behind me. I'm feeling like this is my town. And no chick was off limits to me but (wait a minute) Yolanda, man I've put in a lot of time courting this chick. Plus she's young, fine and pretty, and here I am just coming off a weekend with a call girl, talk about caring for Yolanda, well! I've already answered my question about my loyalty to her. But I still wanted to commit to her. Besides before that weekend I had been real good, and since Fat Cat had come up, I've been chilling taking a break from them bitches. I was just clubbing and hanging with Tubby that didn't seem to bother Yolanda at all. And after countless hours of courting her on the phone and meeting her mom and dad. She was ready to come over to my place. Rony made her feel at home while Fat Cat and I would do our thing, of course we would stop at the liquor store and get something to drink, and would play

Cards and drink until we passed out. And as time went on Fat Cat and Rony got familiar with the city, things were going ok for them. And to my surprise during one of them Friday night drinking parties I had come to know that Rony was also running on a charge, what kind of charge I don't remember, but that blew me away having those kids with her. Made me wonder about this chick, she must have been going through it in her own mind. And she seemed to be handling it well at least on the surface. And out of nowhere she came across somebody who sold cocaine, man! shit has started to get a little crazy around the house. And at this point I had started to see Rony for who she really was, I mean! She continued to be a mom to the kids and she treated me with the same respect, but it was apparent that her and Fat Cat has some issues going on from Baton Rouge, and I think coming here was supposed to be a new start for them. But as always alcohol and drugs unfortunately bring out the worst in people. The coke was a bad idea, I mean! She had all these emotions inside just waiting to come out. Well! It seems Fat Cat had been unfaithful and she had found out I don't remember the details, but it was bad and all I know was here in Seattle he was truly sorry about it. But like they say (hell hath no fury like a woman scorned). And now it seemed to her, "it's game on nigga." And she would do shit just to rub his nose in it. She was determined to fuck him over for what he had done to her. In my mind he was trying to do everything he could to get her to see it differently. But Rony had other ideas. She had met some people and was getting around on her own. It was many times I would take her to the club, hangout and drink dance and she seemed to really enjoy being at the club and we did that and came home.

But like I said she had met people and it was times she went out without me or Fat Cat, and would be gone all night, you could look in Fat Cat's eyes and see that he didn't like that at all. Also it was obvious she wanted him to try something stupid. So he could go to jail, she knew he didn't want that. Man! As long as I've known my cousin I had never known him to take shit like this from a bitch. But this wasn't your average chick; she was different from all the ones I had known. She had that gangsta about her. Also she knows how to be a lady. But for some reason she and I were close, she gave me the respect I felt Fat Cat deserved. But I understood her pain and anger she felt, because of what he did. And I also felt they was in this together. I mean! He's facing prison and she was facing jail time also, you would think they'd come together because of that if nothing else.

But hey! It was beyond repair according to her. Now it's that ghetto drama shit. Well! After all this comes out in the open, I 'm a little hesitant about bringing Yolanda around now. So I go to work, get off come home and get drunk and do it all over again. But how long can I do that, it's not fair to Yolanda or myself. Besides Fat Cat had gotten close to one of the guys at work (Larry). The two of them had this passion for smoking weed and they got close. As for Fat Cat, I felt staying fucked up all the time was his way of dealing with her bullshit. Although I didn't like what was going on, I kind of stayed out of his affair, because I didn't know Rony to judge her and it was obvious he had hurt her deeply.

Besides that, I'm so into Yolanda right now or maybe I just wanted something fresh. Also she made me work for her, I mean! The phone calls, talking to her for hours, making promises I knew I might not keep.

But it felt good to really go after a chick again. She reminded me of the girls back in the day. When you had to work your ass off just to get a kiss. Because now chicks are too easy. I felt good about being with her, someone I could trust. I knew I didn't deserve her love or trust, just look at what I did with the call girl. And to be honest, I didn't see myself changing. And the more I talked to her, I knew! That the right thing to do was to just walk away. First of all, I couldn't tell her the truth about my past, so walking away would have been the right thing to do. But I wasn't known for doing the right thing. Man! The only thing that was going through my mind was that young tender body and that pretty face, that's all I thought about. And when Rony and Fat Cat came to live with me she felt comfortable coming over or maybe it was time, I mean! I had been talking to her for a while now. Besides I was clubbing every weekend and she was too young to get in the clubs so we couldn't do that.

Not only that she was a homebody. So knowing this I wasn't in any kind of hurry to undress her, I had all kinds of chicks for sex. But with her being so shy, she felt like having another woman there would take some of the pressure off her in some way. I'm just saying. I mean! All I know she's ready to be with me man! It's crazy how I'm just like my dad, you know! Like drinking and chasing women and Yolanda she was just like my mom. Putting up with all my bullshit, going to clubs, getting fucked up it didn't bother her at all. To be honest, I didn't know what she saw in me, you see! I talked all that bullshit on the phone about how much I wanted to be with her and all the things I wanted to do for her and last but not least I never wanted to hurt her and when I said those things I really thought I meant it. But after she fell for my shit, "Let's face it that's what it was. I treated her just like the others when I drank.

I got drunk because when I was sober I did all the things I promised, well! She's coming over a lot now, and I'm ready to make love to her and I'm sure she felt the same way I did. Well! I had talked about it on the phone all week it seemed. I mean! I've been patient also I've always respected girls who made me work and wait for them, and Yolanda did that. But it's time and I want her. It would be nice if I could just be sober, because! I feel like I owed her that, after all she wasn't like those other chicks, who just wanted the same thing I wanted. I knew she was different and I want nothing more than to make her feel special. Well! It's Friday and she's coming over tonight, and at work I felt good all day about this weekend. I knew this was the weekend. And just like every other Friday Fat Cat and I went to the liquor store to get our favorite drink, a mixture of cognac and sherry. This was something we had come to do every Friday.

By the way this was something Fat Cat's dad had done with our family on the weekends. And I guess it's something we picked up from him. We love each other like that. Man! By the time Yolanda got to the crib, I was kind of fucked up. Nevertheless she enjoyed being around me no matter how I was, but this was a special night for her and myself. I guess I was just celebrating beforehand, knowing I was going to make this relationship official. Normally when we got through with those two bottles, we would end up getting some coke to bring us down off the alcohol. You see! The cognac and sherry was good but it got you fucked up. And after doing some coke I would end up in the club. But this was a special night so we didn't get any. First of all I didn't want her to see that side of me and another thing I shouldn't be doing coke at all, it's the very thing that got me here in the first place facing 35 years. Anyway as I said, I was feeling good when she came through the door.

And after that I don't remember much. It was morning and waking up looking around in the bed for her, and she's gone, that didn't bother me, she would always be gone. But when I pulled back the sheets there was blood all over the sheet. Man! The first thing I thought about was, what have I done. Honestly I didn't know what happened until I came out of the room, that's when Rony said, how could I have been so insensitive? I had no idea what she was talking about, so I asked her to explain. But first I wanted to know what happened to her because there's blood in my bed. Then Rony said (Herb) she was a virgin, and you should have been gentle with her. But I didn't know she was a virgin, she never said anything to me about being a virgin and also I never asked. I just took for granted that she had been with someone before. Needless to say I rushed to the phone to apologize for being such a jerk off. Man! How and why had I gotten so drunk and not only that, why last night, I asked myself. But I couldn't go back to yesterday, now I

Have to comfort her and tell her how special last night was to me, but to be honest I didn't remember anything about last night, nothing! And I wasn't going to tell her that. Talking to her I could see it meant a lot to her and as for myself I had always wanted a virgin and like her I wanted this experience to be special. But instead of celebrating something as special as this I spent the day trying to figure out how I blew last night. Thinking how could I always get what I want and then somehow, someway screw it up? Nevertheless I must pull myself together and do some damn good acting and do something very special for her. Because the last thing I want to do is let her know that I don't remember much of last night, if anything at all. Well! I'm thinking of something to do for her, but I'm drawing a blank, simply because she is a very simple chick and very easy to please. So it's hard to come up with something.

Well! I got some flowers and a card and on the card I told her how much she means to me and in my mind I couldn't wait until I get her in my bed again. Well! The closer Yolanda and I got it seems that Rony is going all out to make Fat Cat's life a living hell. Doing some crazy shit I knew wasn't right and before now I had been keeping my mouth shut but this was getting crazy, she was leaving on a Friday night and would be gone for two days. This girl had stopped doing their laundry and didn't cook anymore. I just couldn't stand there and watch him act like a pussy, I mean! That wasn't the Fat Cat I had known, I'm thinking what does this bitch want to accomplish by doing this? I knew he loved her, but this was disrespectful and I wanted to know why he wasn't dealing with Rony like he should. And when I asked him about her behavior he would just play it off, like it didn't matter to him. And I would let it go for a time.

But honestly I couldn't be angry with her besides she and I got along really good and when we would be out in the club, she did nothing that I saw was out of line. Maybe she flirted a little; I didn't see anything wrong with that, because I was the same way. But it wouldn't be long before she did this crazy shit again like going out for two nights. And then I confronted him. Yet trying to do it in a respectful manner because! I had tried everything outside of just telling him plainly to confront her about this behavior, yet in spite of my plea for him to say something as he did in the past he just let it go and one Friday night a strange thing happened, just like we did every Friday we stopped at the liquor store and got our favorite drinks. And on this night we had gotten some damn good coke. I think Larry and someone else had come by to bullshit, I mean! We had a ball as we often did. So here I am drunk and high on coke, I decided I wanted to put the bartender chick to the test.

And I had a role for Rony to play. I came up with this plan to see if she cared for me. The plan was to get money out of her for more coke that night (sick shit I know). And I thought it was fool proof, it was up to Rony to pull this shit off, she had to call the chick on the phone and tell her I'm in jail and I needed her to give Rony the bail money and Rony was coming to get me out since she was at work. And to my surprise she was willing to bail me out, but it was one thing I didn't think about and that was, what if she wanted to come herself. And guess what, that's just what happened. Not only was that one of the most heartless things I've ever done knowing for sure that she really cared for me made it almost impossible for me to see her again. But as always I came to her with an excuse. But nevertheless I could tell she never fully trusted me again. But we remained friends though I didn't deserve it. And another thing that surprised me that night was that Rony was so down with me.

Willing to stoop that low, now it was her turn to do something just as fucked up. Well! I remember it as though it was yesterday. Fat Cat and I stopped by the liquor store one Friday, but this night Fat Cat had gotten real fucked up and passed out on the couch, I mean! Fucked up like someone had put something in his drink and for some reason I wasn't wasted, oh! Don't get me wrong I was high and feeling good but not fucked up. Rony was loaded and kind of stumbling around and I asked her if she was alright and she asked me to help her to the bedroom. And while laying her down on the bed, she put her arms around my neck out of the blue trying to kiss me. Pulling me closer to her, all I could say was no that's my cousin I can't do this, and I meant that and she tried her best to lay with me. But Fat Cat was closer than a brother. I would never do that to him. And I walked away and the next day I had forgotten all about it.

And it was over as far as I'm concerned, but to my surprise she was pissed off with me, as if I had done something wrong. Nevertheless I would just play it off, but she began to do thing that was obvious to me that she didn't appreciate my decision to reject whatever that was she tried to pull. I didn't regret it either, but we are grown folks and besides we have to live together for now anyway. Well! Rony at this time had become very good friends with a white chick (Shelley). Very pretty but over weight, ok fat (it is what it is). And it was obvious that Rony was very fond of Shelley and Shelley was warm and very nice. She also had a kid and her and Rony had a lot in common. Thank God for Shelley because it took some of the tension away that was between Rony and myself. But wait a minute it created another dilemma for me, Shelley had it bad for me and I wasn't into her at all, as a friend yes she was cool and when she came over and the drinks were flowing and of course a little powder sometimes and we just talk shit all night.

While playing cards or some other game. But to sleep with her, I didn't even consider that, to me she was just cool people and I knew she had it bad for me and I played it for everything its worth, like talking real smooth shit to her and that was as far as I would go with it. Besides she had seen the chicks coming in and out of my bed. So I had no need to sleep with her. Yolanda was my main girl; Shelley knew that, c'mon I have nothing against big bitches but man! How would that look, me sleeping with Shelley? When I have this young fine ass chick that loves me. But that didn't stop this chick. And as a player you have to respect that part of the game. I should fuck her just on that alone. But (hey) I'm a gambler; let's see how far she'll go I mean I got nothing to lose anyway. (By the way) I think Rony was really pushing this. Well! One day Shelley called and invited me over for dinner, my first thought was no, then again (what the fuck) it can't hurt, it's only dinner.

So I said sure I'll be glad to have dinner with you. Man! I'll never forget that night. Don't get me wrong it was a very nice dinner, she had cooked a great Italian meal and it was prepared beautifully and the wine was good, and here's the kicker, after dinner she asked me to watch a movie with her and there's nothing wrong with dinner and a movie (right)? So she puts the movie in and bam! It's a porno flick.

And that when I said I have something very important to do. Man! That was very clever of her, but I got the fuck out of there and quick. Needless to say! She kept trying but I kept saying no. But Shelley wasn't taking no for an answer, well one night we was getting fucked up, it wasn't' anything special, we was just doing what we do (I guess). Anyway! Shelley was over, matter of fact all kinds of people was there, I mean! We were playing cards, whatever! So it was no different from any other Friday night.

Well! So I thought, the last thing I remember I was telling people good night and then waking up in the morning and feeling around in the bed and to my surprise pulling the cover back and it's Shelley telling me morning and about the night of sex we had. Needless to say my first response was (you gotta be kidding me). To be honest, I didn't know how she got in my bed and if I had sex with her and at the end of the day I knew she was going to try anything to be with me, Needless to say! Fat Cat and the guys at worked teased me forever about it. It was all good. Well! In Spite of all my wild weekends of drinking and sometimes coke. Yolanda was happy and in love and not only that we are having sex every time she's over to the crib and she has no idea what's going on when she's not around. Besides she's not an emotional person in the first place, so it's hard to tell what's going on in her head.

And to be honest I'm not too concerned about my behavior when she's not around. I mean! I'm giving her everything I think she may want. And at the same time Rony and Fat Cat are going through it big time. Finally one night I got all in his shit about her treating him this way. Of course I was fucked up and somehow we ended up fighting in the hallway of the apartment. It didn't do any good, he still defended her. Well! The only good thing about the whole thing was they ended up moving out and getting a place in the same building where Shelley lived. I know he was mad at me about that night, but I didn't think too much about it. Then again I knew it was Rony pushing his buttons because on that night of the fight, I kind of put it all out there, like how I felt about his situation and what I thought he should do about that bitch. But that shit backfired and this nigga seemed to love this bitch even more. Maybe I should've just kept acting as if I didn't care.

Who knows, (it's strange!). In spite of everything that has happened, I did end up missing them a little. But as they say life goes on, and I turned my attention to my girl and I started having her over almost every night and I was cool with that and as fate would have it, it wasn't too long before Fat Cat and myself would be back together as cousins and friends. But they never came back to visit and I never went over to visit them either. Well! I had gotten hurt at work, ok! What happen was, we had to keep the walk way clear because in the process of sorting through the paper the walk way would fill up with paper so we had to keep it clean, and how we kept it clean was to take turns kicking the paper down the walkway and at times it would be all kinds of trash inside the pile as we kicked it. And when it was my turn to clean the walkway, while kicking through the paper I kicked a large can of some kind and it just happened to be the leg with the iron rod in it from the car accident. Somehow it got infected and of course I had to take some time off and have surgery.

While I'm off from work, I'm waiting on the workman's comp and in the meantime I'm living off my savings account and while going to the bank I was friends with all the tellers and every time I went in there it was this one teller who would always flirt with me and I never thought about it too much. Hey! I've flirted with her every time I went in that bank but never anything serious. But being off from work because of the injury, I went to the bank more often than I had been before the accident. I had a chance to see her more often, so we talked on occasion and one day we were talking she said she was thinking about going back home to Laramie, WY. And before I knew it I had asked her to dinner, not knowing if she had a boyfriend or if she was married or whatever. But to my surprise she said "yes." But we didn't set a day for the date. And I never thought about it too much, and the more I went into the bank the more she seemed to tell me a little something about herself.

Now! I'm thinking what's with this girl. I mean! I had been banking here ever since I got the job at the recycle center. And I had told them all the crazy shit that was happening in my life, etc. Man! They knew about the girls, I didn't hide anything from them; of course I didn't talk about my past. But work and my weekend clubbing I didn't mind telling them about that. And for her to still ask me to go out with her, I didn't see anything wrong with that. But before we went out I had noticed when I came into the bank the other girls would say something to me about (Chris), things like you guys would make a great couple, and if I came into the bank and she was in the back, someone would go get her. Man! I still didn't trip, I mean! She was going back to wherever, besides! She knew I had been with my young chick and whoever else. Yet she still wanted to go out. And also I made it clear I wasn't promising her anything, whatever happens just happens. It means nothing and that's the way I was. And still she was ok with me. That's when I knew she wanted more than dinner and I didn't have a problem giving her whatever she wanted. To be honest I've always wanted to spend a night or sometime with her, she was always so nice to me, no matter what kind of mood I was in when I went into the bank, she made me feel better. So for her to want to be with me or just to have dinner meant a lot to me. And to my surprise I was looking forward to going to dinner with her. And I didn't know if it would be one date or one hundred, I wanted this one to be special after all she was going back to Wyoming. And not knowing if I would ever see her again, so I was determined to make sure she have a good time while she was with me also she didn't know when she was leaving. So I thought on the first date, I would take her to a Sonic's basketball game and after that dinner. Well! I got up with X McDaniel and got some good tickets. Well! Finally we have a day and we're going on this long awaited date and after meeting her after work, walking to my place talking, she's more interesting than I ever thought, she was very easy to talk to and she was ready to see the game and there was one thing she wanted me to know she wanted me to know that she had a boyfriend but they had broken up a few months ago. Honestly I didn't care about that, I had Yolanda and I made it clear from the beginning about that. Besides I had too many girls already, but I didn't see anything wrong with going out with her or any other chick. And also she was a Mormon and although I wasn't following my faith at that time, but I had respect for all religion. Though I didn't know much about her faith and religion. I kind of thought they didn't date outside of their race. Needless to say! I had lots of questions (but not tonight).

It was time for letting go of the everyday distraction, and enjoy the moment. Besides I was enjoying her company and of course the cognac makes things a little easier. And during the game she said never mind dinner let's just go to your place. Well I'm feeling good from the drinks and I was down for whatever, needless to say she got what she wanted and after that night we was together until she went back to Wyoming. Wow! I didn't see this coming, she wanted to give up her place and stay with me until she left. Hey! I was cool with it, but I got a girlfriend, she was easy, but I would have to come up with some bullshit story to keep her away. But this wasn't a day or two. This was maybe two weeks, three weeks, four I just didn't know and I didn't want to ask. All I knew was when I got home from work she was there cooking dinner in something sexy and I knew I only had her for a short time. Nor was I going to waste a minute.

So we spend the rest of her time in Seattle making love, laughing and talking, getting to know each other. Basically enjoying each other's company. Honestly I felt good around her. I took her to more Sonic games although McDaniel was tripping because I had never asked him for two tickets before. He knew how I played them chicks, and what really fucked him up, was I wasn't coming to the club and that wasn't like me at all, man! I was always at the club. Needless to say this was strange even to me, I mean! I knew I didn't love her or anything like that, it's just being with her it was so peaceful and maybe I needed some peace. Not only that it was just two people enjoying one another and when she leaves it would be over. It was a beautiful thing. Man! I remember how she looked forward to going to college and getting her degree. And I was truly happy for her and my wish for her was to have a wonderful life. And one day she was gone. Well! I wasn't surprised that she had left but what surprised me was I had felt something for this girl.

But that wasn't reality Yolanda was and is my future. Now I just have to put the last few weeks behind me and call Yolanda. Needless to say she was more than ready to take her place and somehow I didn't feel bad about putting her on hold. You would think I should, knowing how much she loved me. But when it came down to me and some other woman I was always willing to get her in my bed. And in Seattle it seemed like women came a dime a dozen. I'm not saying that in a slimy way. But really sex was easy to get in Seattle, and for me I wanted my share knowing it could be the last girl I'll see in a while, because of my situation with the law. And while Yolanda and I was getting back to normal I told myself from now on its just going to be me and her. (Think about it) I felt I was playing it close bringing chicks to my crib and not only that keeping her away for weeks sometimes. And then coming up with these lame ass excuses. And it's been about two months since Chris has left and Yolanda and I are doing good as always.

And one day I got a call from Chris telling me she was carrying our child, and she was sorry. Well! I didn't know what to say and in my heart I wanted to do the right thing, but the timing wasn't right for this. Man! I'm running from the law and besides I'm loving Yolanda. Man! I needed to think about this also I didn't know her that well. But it's a baby that's involved now am I going to do her like I did the others or am I going to commit? Well! We're talking almost every day now and I wanted to have her here with me, but I just didn't know her and in my heart I knew she was good people but with 30 years hanging over my head I couldn't put her through that. Well! There's one person I needed to talk to about this and I knew she would tell me what to do, and that's my grandmother. So I called my grandmother and explained to her what had happened here with this wonderful woman.

And I didn't know what to do and I explained to my grandmother that it was more than one girl involved. I wasn't in love with the one who's carrying the child I needed some time to think this over. Don't get me wrong the last thing I wanted to do was to leave another woman hanging not only that but hanging with a child. At the same time if and when I'm caught I'll end up leaving her anyway. Besides I had so much invested in Yolanda, she was also very important to me. Should I just toss her aside? Well, after listening to me my grandmother said, "Baby go with your heart." My heart was telling me to leave her where she's at. My life was just too damn complicated to bring her here with me, but how am I to tell her to stay there where she's at because it's best you see. I'm running from the law. I just couldn't bring myself to tell her the truth. I try and tell myself to do it. I just don't want her caught up in all this shit. Well, sometime had passed and I wanted to talk to her just to see how she's doing.

As you can imagine she didn't want to have anything to do with me. After all I had stood her up and left her there and that would be the end of us and the end of me trying to talk to her. Being a better human being than I was she kept in touch with my mother. She sent her pictures of the baby. It was a beautiful little girl.

Chapter 15

It Is What It Is —
I Want What I Want

I'm all healed up and ready to go back to work. When I
got back on a Monday morning, the company had hired
some new people and one of them happened to be Rickey's
sister-in-law and one of the guys was his brother-in-law.
The other guy was a friend of Rickey's. Three new people.
At first I didn't think that much about the girl. But when we
went to lunch she had taken off some of her clothes and her
hard hat. I found her to be rather attractive, but it couldn't
be more than that because Yolanda and I were doing well
in spite of my whatever you call it with Chris. I kept my
thoughts to myself.

As we worked together on the line we started to do silly
stuff like throw paper at each other. Supposedly we were
throwing it when the other one wasn't looking. We had so
much fun bullshitting on that line. It was unreal. We would
come up with all kinds of one liners on that line and not
only that you wouldn't believe the items we would find as

we sorted the paper. Things like clothes, toys, cologne, etc. The clothes came from major department stores. After the holidays when the public would take these things back to the department stores that was the time we would take back the items we found for either exchange or refund. This was a good place in my life. The three people hired while I was off proved to be a welcomed edition to the already wonderful cast of characters we had already.

Doc was one and Van was the other and last but not least the girl Jeanne'. Doc and Jeanne' were connected in two ways. Doc's dad was the brother of Jeanne's mother and when her mother suddenly passed away he adopted Jeanne' and her sister, who by the way was Rickey's wife. Van was close friends of both Doc and Jeanne'. Doc's whole family had worked there and most of them were still working there.

Cain, Van and myself had gotten close. We started going to the tavern together. Doc and Van loved to throw darts. That was something I had never played. I've always enjoyed doing new things. At work all of us would go to lunch together. Doc and I would talk mostly because we were about the same age. Also, he was the only one that would have a beer with me. As time went by we became a close group.

It was obvious that I was getting close to Jeanne'. At lunch I would find myself spending a lot of time with her, or maybe it was all in my mind. After all she was a very outgoing and friendly person. Plus everyone knew about Yolanda and Jeanne' was married but she was separated. As time went on she would say things to me about being with such a young girl as she would say (putting emphasis on young girl). At first I would play it off and just laugh, but apparently she wasn't playing at all. She would say, "You need a grown woman!" And that a woman like herself could give me more than Yolanda ever could. I must admit, I wasn't' totally pleased with being with just Yolanda or maybe it was just the idea of being with one woman. I loved her and I would do almost anything for her, but she was young and she didn't have any street smarts and that hood chick kind of thing that I like.

Jeanne' was right on and the more she and I talked the more I wanted to experience her. She just took me there to that place with a woman I always wanted to go. As we talked about all the things we both enjoyed God we were so much alike. Wait a minute, I have this woman who is in love with me and whom I care about. Besides I had put a ring on her finger and at the same time I am making her into the woman I wanted. Yet and still I wasn't totally satisfied with her. Maybe I wanted too much too soon or maybe I didn't know what I wanted. When Jeanne' came along I thought I was over the bullshit and done with it. It was Yolanda past present and future, PERIOD! I thought I was confused before but man! I knew it was wrong thinking about Jeanne' but that never stopped me in the past and it seems like I wasn't about to let that stop me now. For some reason I just want what I want and now it seems I want Jeanne'.

Maybe I could have her and still keep my love for Yolanda intact. I wonder was it just a physical thing with Jeanne'? If that's the case that's all it'll be and nobody gets hurt. Besides Jeanne' knew how I felt about Yolanda. She knows Yolanda was a virgin and what that meant to me. We talked about that kind of thing at work, so I knew she knew that it could be nothing but sex between us. That's how I saw it. There was no doubt in my mind that's how it would be. If I go down this road I need to be clear with Jeanne' about this.

As we talked she was also clear about her situation. It was no turning back for her. Her marriage was over, but in his mind he wanted his wife back. In spite of moving out of their house he had hope that she would want him back. To me this was a typical love story in the hood or anywhere else for that matter. Over time we put all the cards on the table. At this point all we had was a real good working relationship and I was cool with that.

Who am I kidding? Inside of me I was yearning for her and for the most part I kept it to myself. But she had to know how I was feeling, we ate lunch together and I made it my business to work on her side of the line. I wanted to be close to her every chance I got. Well! It is just one thing I need to do, and it's my way of seeing if she's the one for me or if it's just in my head. And that was the kiss, (I mean) the vibe was there. The conversations and the touching, but to me, it's in the kissing. The passion it brings (man)! It's a must because if I'm going to betray this girl again, it has to be a very passionate affair. By now I'm tired of thinking about it. I must go out on a limb and kiss this girl. So at lunch one day I call her into the bathroom and took her by the hand and kissed her. Needless to say it was everything I thought it would be and more.

Wow! The passion was so strong between us, and from that day on...she was mine. You see this wasn't a knock on Yolanda or to take anything away from her. She was good for me, and I cared for her deeply, but what I saw in Jeanne' was what I've always sought in a woman — edgy, smart, classy and hood, I wanted to experience her even at the price of losing Yolanda and even having to deal with her husband. Either way I wanted her, and to get this ball rolling I had just the thing, it would be a candle lit dinner with wine at my crib. Oh! How can I forget about the music-Luther, Marvin to help me with this night. I wanted it to be a night she would never forget. She was everything I thought she would be and more. Man! The passion was incredible. It seemed like this night could last forever. Also the view of the skyline of the city from my living room window was insane.

It was no doubt we enjoyed every moment of this evening. In the morning, I still felt the passion for her, just like that first kiss. But, there is one thing I have to consider and it won't be easy. I have to take a moment to think about this, is it love or lust. C'mon, I've put in a lot of time with Yolanda besides I've taken her through a lot of bullshit, and now I've come to love her and she loves me as well in spite of all my bullshit. Well! Jeanne' wants me to know she is very sure that she didn't want her husband anymore and it's over between them. But, with me it was different. Yolanda was the perfect girl for me. Wow! I fucked up. I thought it would be just sex, and now it's like I met my soul mate. Ok. Just think (Herb) she knows what kind of nigga I am. She's just going to have to accept Yolanda being in my life, and it seems she does.

To my surprise, I'm the one who wants more because on our lunch break I would take her into this bathroom and we would have sex. I would find myself wining and dining her two or three nights a week. Needless to say telling Yolanda all kinds of bullshit excuses to keep her away, and it went well for months. To keep Yolanda happy, she had two or three days a week with me. Hey! I'm in Seattle, it's my own little heaven. It's going my way everybody is happy. (Not only that) I have this credit account at this jewelry store. Whatever I bought for Yolanda, when things would get a little crazy with Jeanne' I would buy the same thing for her. I figured if Yolanda loved it, she would too. That was the easy part. Now, the question is how long will this go on this way. Well! I'm about to see, because Jeanne' is about to show her ass. Ok! She seems to think Yolanda is a problem now.

This didn't start until I went and stayed overnight at her house. It was obvious we were sleeping together. Everyone at work knew how much I cared about Yolanda, and at this point in our relationship she didn't like it when guys asked me about Yolanda. I guess meeting her kids and staying overnight really meant something to her, but as for me it was business as usual. Even though Jeanne' and I had so much in common, the passion and all the things I wanted in a woman she had it. But, to hurt Yolanda really weighed heavy on my mind, and I was determined to think it through. Man! The last thing I wanted to do was hurt Yolanda or Jeanne' they both were good to me. But just like the ones before them someone was going to get hurt. I wanted them both, and in my mind I was going to make it work.

It would turn out to be harder than I thought. I worked with Jeanne' and she had the upper hand just because of that. Wait! Shit has just started to get crazy around here, her husband has found out that she's seeing someone and he isn't going down without a fight, but I quickly found out, he was the kind of nigga that would not confront the guy, but he would make her life a living hell. Example — one night I slept over at her house and she insisted that I park in her garage. We had been out shooting pool and I had a real good time eating and drinking and the next morning I get up to find that my tires were on a flat. Well! That didn't bother me as much as she not telling me that this nigga had a key to the house. Man! I didn't like being put in a situation like that. Needless to say! I was pissed off with her (not only that) I made her get me new tires. Maybe I should have walked away then, but I couldn't, I had come to care for her.

Besides, Yolanda made it too easy for me to do this kind of shit. Hey! Yolanda asked no questions and I wasn't offering any apology. And besides I still treated her good in spite of spending most of my time with Jeanne'. Also Jeanne' went out of her way to win my heart by doing the things I wanted Yolanda to do, like coming over to the crib cooking dinner, all kinds of surprises, even taking me to dinner, taking me to the movies, doing the things I had once enjoyed doing (not only that) her kids were infatuated with California and mainly Compton, with the whole rap thing going on, and I had a lot of that Compton swagger going on at that time. So the kids and I got along real good. Of course that made Jeanne' happy to know that her kids accept me. But, still to even think about walking away from Yolanda was hard and will be something I would struggle with the next few months.

But in my heart I knew I was feeling Jeanne' and it was unfair to Yolanda because I knew she didn't have anything to offer right now. I mean! She was only eighteen, and also I was her first love. No doubt it was going to be a process with her, but at the same time Jeanne' was already where I wanted her to be, and she made everything a little easy. But still it wasn't going to be easy. I was going to hurt one of these beautiful women, and working with Jeanne' made it easy for me to love her. Well! Yolanda was beginning to notice something was going on with me, and it was a few times she had come over, and it was obvious that she had been drinking. Pleading with me not to leave her and my heart went out to her. Needless to say! I told her she was wrong thinking something like that and I would never leave her. I kissed her and held her, and made love to her. Never the less I was surprised because before that night she had never showed any kind of emotion. I had never seen her angry. Just that beautiful smile, I mean she hardly ever expresses herself, never I love you. Oh! She would answer when I asked her things like do you love me, but that was it. For her to come over and show this side of her, I was deeply touched. But maybe it was too late, and I say this in respect for her, because I held on as best as I could to the both of them, but Jeanne' made it easy in spite of her punk ass husband. I stayed over at her house more and more, and it was clear to me I'm feeling Jeanne' more that Yolanda.

Chapter 16

Oh Shit! It's Getting Hot in Here

Well! One night Jeanne' was over at my crib and out of nowhere there's a knock on the door, and needless to say it's Yolanda. In my mind I'm thinking (oh shit!) why are you here. I had not seen her this way/ maybe it was just her being a woman knowing there's another woman around. Of course I had never been this involved with any of the others. I guess you could say she wanted to size up the chick, and no doubt she had some choice words for me, and I understood that I had never let it come to this and I just knew she would just walk away and I was ready for that. Matter of fact I would have preferred that because what was about to happen I wasn't ready for it. Instead of her walking out she wanted me to choose, and I still wasn't ready to let go of either one of them.

I pleaded with her to just leave so I could deal with Jeanne', and then Jeanne' had something to say as well. While I was trying to keep Jeanne' quiet I could tell she had noticed the jewelry that Yolanda had on. Of course it was the same as what she has. Man! It got crazy and it was hard to see that the woman I said I love standing there crying, and I didn't comfort her, and not only that I asked her to walk away and I'll deal with this in the morning. She just left telling me to make a decision and soon. After she left I went on with my plan to have dinner with Jeanne'. I'll deal with this soon. In spite of the shit that went on that night I just kept playing with the both of them. It had gotten like some high school shit. Lord knows I knew someone would get hurt, and I knew it was so wrong of me to do this, but I just couldn't let neither one go. Well! Jeanne' was beginning to put my hands to the fire, by doing stupid shit, like not calling me and missing work just to fuck with my mind, and guess what it's working. I found myself wondering where she's at while I'm with Yolanda. Until she started doing this shit, I really didn't know how much I cared for her. Nevertheless it wouldn't be too long before Yolanda came over again finding Jeanne' there.

As before, confronting me about Jeanne' and telling me to leave Jeanne' alone. Man! I could tell by the look in her eyes it was all or nothing for her at this point. Well! In all honesty I didn't want her to walk out that door because I Knew I wasn't going to see her again. But, I felt in my heart Jeanne' was where I wanted to be at this point in my life. Of course I've been wrong before and if I'm wrong this time, I would say this would be the biggest mistake I've made as far as a relationship with a woman is concerned. Hey! I've made all kinds of stupid mistakes in my life and this one will be right up there with the best. I'll tell you the truth, it broke my heart to watch her beg me, and having to physically put her out of the apartment was an all-time low for even me. After she had gone, I realize I did that with Jeanne' right there watching. How cold was that telling her to leave?

Man! If she had just walked away it would have been different maybe. But for me to stand there and make her beg me. Oh God! I still hate myself for that- Hearing her in the hall crying. But at the time I thought I did the right thing. Hey, Yolanda is young she'll be okay, but in Jeanne' I've found my soul mate. I was falling in love with Jeanne' and she was in love with me. After Yolanda had gone there was only one person who was happy and no doubt that's Jeanne'. Somehow I went back to my evening with her and that was the end of Yolanda. I must admit it was strange in the weeks following that night, knowing in my heart that Yolanda will no longer be a part of my life. But I had made a decision, and I just got to believe that I made the right one. To be honest it wasn't a right or a wrong decision here. It was the fact that I was hurting someone who cared about me very much.

This kind of behavior has become a way of life for me. Since Jeanne' and I were close in age and we respect each other a lot. Last but not least we had so much passion between us and it was obvious when we were together, and that's one of the reasons I felt okay about my future with Jeanne', and knowing Yolanda would find someone to love her and just her. So I turn my attention to building a future with Jeanne' and her kids. No sooner than we are putting the whole Yolanda thing behind us here comes her husband and acting a fool by making her life hard mostly concerning their kids. It was like the closer she and I got the more angry he got. She had said as long as she is alone he didn't come around. But when someone comes along this nigga would act an ass, but that's what niggas do (we don't want her, until she wants to move on, and it was no different for him). I wasn't getting in his way, she's going to have to get out of this shit herself as far as I was concerned. Besides she was still in their house, and as long as she was staying in their house, I guess he had a right to do what he was doing. Even though I loved her, I didn't want her and him. Besides I had had some experience in the past with this type of shit and also I was sure that she loved me and somehow she was handling the situation correctly. Lastly it has to work out I had let Yolanda walk away and now my future was with this chick. I just wanted her to handle this dude the right way so there would be no looking back, just her and myself. Needless to say, he wouldn't go away that easy because the more time she spent with me the more he wanted her back and not only that she seems to be falling for that bullshit.

Man at times I question my decision to be with her, but at the same time while we were at work, I was (like) telling her to give him the opportunity to get his family back even though I didn't mean it, but I felt I needed to say it. Maybe to see if she had any kind of doubt about us before we go any farther. Man! I just wanted to settle down with her, this is my soul mate. But I'll be lying if I said there weren't any issues in the beginning, because there were and at this point I was willing to fight for her. Shit man! This cat made more money than I did and as we know money solves all kinds of problems. I couldn't compete with him on the money side, but I knew she loved me and maybe that would be enough. Besides she loved the way I treated her, so I continued to offer her candle lit dinners, the whole nine yards. I know one thing for sure, he couldn't compete with that.

So I just kind of stepped back and let the chips fall where they may, and if she decided to give her marriage one last shot, and she did and needless to say I was scared I would lose her. Man! This nigga was doing the right things, from bringing her to and from work, flowers the whole nine. I was sick when I saw that, but I kept my head up and we continued to work together, and of course we ate lunch with each other. Needless to say I was pretty sure of myself. It was all up to her and her alone. Well! It would be about a month or so before it was over between them.

Chapter 17

Just Us...Me and My Soul mate

Apparently she had moved out of their home, and gotten her a little three bedroom place, before she had come to see me about a future together. Even though she was still married legally, but in my heart she was mine now, and her getting this place meant that she was leaving the past behind and moving forward, and she wanted me to be a part of that. Of course I wanted that as well. Finally, I am where I want to be and also at work everything's good. At home we are doing well. But as in the past, my drinking has somehow taken on a life of its own, and I don't understand why. C'mon I have my soul mate, the girl I've always wanted, and not only that a good job. Well! I could blame Doc because every since he came on board we've drank on our lunch break, but I won't. No one made me drink, but still I didn't drink at lunch before he came, and I could have but I chose not to. So the choice was mine and mine alone. So now I just need to get a hold of it and fast. Somehow I manage to pull myself together, and Jeanne' and I became strong as a couple. By this time she and the husband had worked out some type of deal concerning the kids.

Now it's just Jeanne' and I for the most part. The two boys were with their dad and the girl who was about fourteen was with her dad. It was the perfect situation at this time, and we decided to get an apartment together in Tukwila just south of Seattle. Not only that I wanted a new car, I had credit, but being on the run I couldn't use my real name, because I didn't want to get a license being on the run had me trapped in my own mind. You see, here I am with the perfect girl for me, and knowing I could have it all taken away at any time. Now the thought of this was beginning to wear on me once again. And once again drinking was the thing I turned to just to numb the pain. I mean normally I would run away at this point, but not this time, this girl. I want to be with her, but the thought of getting caught and never seeing her again was almost too much to bear.

It seems between drinking and thinking, I'm hoping I'm somewhere in the middle with this, but then again something is telling me to get the fuck out of here, but at the same time I'm getting in deeper and deeper. I'm thinking about buying a new car and putting it in her name. Hey! We've already gotten this nice crib together. Nevertheless in my mind I'm going crazy because in my heart I want to tell her everything about my past, because clearly there is a change going on with me. The drinking, the mood swings, etc. Man! After being here, having friends, a real good job, but it's still no one I felt I could confide in, and having this secret life had worked me down in the beginning, but I managed to weather that storm, and just when I thought I was over this, here I am again. But this time it's different. I'm in love and it hasn't been that long of a relationship and I've already invested so much into this girl.

I've brought the car knowing it could be over at any time. So now I'm thinking, should I give my all to her or what? Or maybe I'll just take it day by day as I said before I'm in too deep to just give up now. Well! Maybe buying the car and having the crib could be enough to keep my head in the game or do I leave right now. I've lost all kinds of shit before. Okay, forget about me, what about her, what's going to happen to her when I'm caught, what's that going to do to her, is she going to feel betrayed because I did not tell her what I'm facing and somehow I got to deal with this storm in my head. Well in the beginning I was on the right track, arriving here in Seattle with a plan. Now look how far I've come, wow! The church seems so far behind me. Well

I could go and share with them what I'm going through at this point.

I don't think so, because I didn't when I had the chance. Anyway I feel it's too late, I could tell I was going down, but I love her enough to try and keep it together, but my drinking was king and it seem at the most important time in my life it would reign and take over and make me a slave to it as always. It has its way with me and somehow I self-destruct. So it was just a matter of time before I came tumbling down. But I wasn't going to give up, how you fight against yourself. So in my own crazy way I tried to tell her I was going through something. Well! Instead of telling her in words being the crazy dude that I am, I'm acting out and it's all wrong. Sometime it's anger and then again sometimes it's pure joy when I'm with her. No doubt it leads to her being confused, because here I am the guy of her dreams, after all we went through.

Yolanda, her husband and now here I am dealing with my past again. Imagine, I went from candle lit dinners, bubble baths, and flowers to acting like someone who cares about nothing or no one. But in my heart I want her and if only I could get these charges to go away because the more I loved her, the more I see those thirty years. Besides my life on the run in Seattle has been a rollercoaster ride filled with ups and downs, highs and lows. After all I'm only human and one could only take so much of this emotional rollercoaster ride. Maybe that's just what I'm going through. Well! One day I had been out drinking and I came home and started all kinds of bullshit. Not only that I said it was time for me to leave and go back to Los Angeles because it was the place for me. I told her I was sorry for leading her to believe we had a future together.

So if you don't mind I'll just take my car and go. Well, of course she didn't want to hear none of that. Come on! I was tripping man! Shit I was running from California as well as Louisiana. It seems I couldn't get away from hurting her. If I leave I was going to hurt her and if I stayed I would end up getting caught and being taken away from her and hurting her. Wow! I was going to hurt her either way. Nevertheless, I continued to make our life at home difficult as well as at work. Mentally I was self-destructing and a few times I wanted to tell her what I was going through, after all! It had a lot to do with her. Knowing that I didn't want to leave her, but I knew I was mentally drained, so I continued to try and push her away, but she was just as stubborn as I am, and when I came home with an attitude she was very smart, so she would do something nice for me.

Man! Something inside of me wanted to come clean and when I couldn't I knew it was time to leave Seattle. To think my life was complicated before this chick came along, it was really confusing now and in spite of what I was going through, Jeanne' and I really loved each other, and that passion we had at the beginning was still there. But the thought of being here with her for three, five, ten years and then getting caught would be something I don't think I could handle. I mean if I didn't love her so much, maybe I'll feel differently. But it is what it is and the thought of not seeing her again was just too hard. So in my twisted state of mind, I just continued to make being with me a little harder each day. After a night of throwing darts and drinking heavy, I somehow convince myself it was time to go. Needless to say she didn't want to hear that bullshit again.

After she and I talked all night she managed to calm me down and talk me out of leaving. She didn't want to give up the car, but even after sleeping it off my mind was made up.

A few days later at work I started a fight with her and that led to both of us getting fired. I knew she wasn't coming home that night, shit with the way I was acting. I was out of my mind it seemed. Talking about leaving and all kinds of stupid shit. Honestly I can't say why I acted that way. I knew she didn't deserve to be left in the dark and treating her this way was wrong but I didn't know what was right anymore. Since I've been here in Seattle I've managed to hurt three (3) women that cared about me. After two (2) or three (3) days she comes home. I've been drinking, of course but this time I'm calm and trying to tell her that I love her and that I must leave. I do so without giving any reason for my needing to leave.

I'm not making any sense at all to her at this point. I've gone too far to turn back. She's crying and asking me what's wrong. All I would tell her was that I just have to leave, that I just had to get away. She's begging me to stay at this point, telling me how much she loves me. I knew she didn't want me to go or take the car from her. I knew she could stop me from taking the car. She is confused about this turn of events. She just kept asking why. I had no answers for her because the only answer there was, was the truth and I wasn't about to tell her that.

Chapter 18

Here I am Front and Center With My Past.

Tonight's the night and nothing is going to stop me. I'm packing, she's crying. She's telling me to wait and let's talk about it in the morning. As far as I was concerned there's no more talking. As she's pleading with me I'm trying to take the car keys from her but this was to no avail. She would not give me those keys. I became frustrated and I started throwing shit around and yelling all the while she's still crying. The situation was going nowhere. I took her hand and I tried to grab the keys from it. Somehow she managed to get outside. She tried to leave in the car. Well I'm drunk and stupid so I stood in front of the car to stop her from leaving. I could have sworn she would've run over me if I hadn't gotten out of the way at the last second. Apparently she went to a phone somewhere because she came back to the apartment a little while later and she had some friends with her (police).

Here I am front and center with my past and somehow I managed to stay calm. They took her outside to talk to her while I was in the apartment. Well it was two police officers that took her outside and two that stayed inside with me. The two inside with me began questioning me asking, "What's wrong and why are you doing this?" All the while I could hear her outside saying to the other policemen, "I don't want him to leave or anything like that. I just want him to calm down and talk to me." After talking with both of us they got my name. Man! I just knew I was busted that night. They asked her to leave mainly because she had the car and then they left. I couldn't believe they walked out of the apartment without me. I didn't know how it happened but somehow I'd escaped that night. Man! That was close! My God. I've got to sober up and get my shit together. I wasn't looking for them to come back tonight or the next night and besides I needed this time to figure out what was important to me. Should I stay and tell her the truth? At this point my worst fear has come and gone. A run in with the law and they missed me, after everyone is gone I decided to take a shower and get some sleep.

I just kept thinking she had the cops come over to where I live and over some bullshit. Tomorrow I'm going to talk to her and make this shit right again. That's what I'll do.

Tomorrow couldn't get here fast enough. I'm not looking for her to come home anytime soon. Last night seemed like it would never end. I'm just ready to get back to myself and live life, make every day count for something, just like I did when I first got here. I could do that. I did it before. I really wanted to call her but instead I decided she was probably pissed and it was just best to wait. Besides she'll call me eventually.

It's the next day and I'm hung over. I have nothing to do and cant' go anywhere because she has the car. Well, I'll just eat and watch TV. The day is almost spent and no phone call from Jeanne' as I expected. Just as I was getting ready for bed, the phone rang. I was somewhat surprised. I knew it was too soon for Jeanne' to be calling me but still I raced to the phone. When I got there no one was on the other end. I thought maybe she was just checking to see if I was still here. I mean I was supposed to be leaving. As I crawled back into bed the phone rang again. Just as before no one is there. I really thought it was Jeanne' again. I went back to bed and turn on the TV. The phone rang again. This time I said to myself, "I'm not playing this game." I refused to get up again.

I started falling asleep and then there was a knock on the door. I thought to myself where is her key? I went to answer the door and to my surprise it's the cops from the other night. At that moment it seemed my world stopped. The first thing the woman cop said was, "The apartment is surrounded." Well I wasn't running away. I thought to myself finally it's over. It was bittersweet of course and even more so because I didn't get a chance to tell Jeanne' the truth. I really wanted to know why they didn't arrest me the night before.

The lady cop in charge of the investigation told me that they had to be sure I was the right Herbert Lawson, III. They were waiting on my picture from Port Allen PD. Once they got it there was no question I was who Port Allen PD was looking for. They had someone posted up at the apartment building all day and night anyway so I wouldn't have been able to leave. In my head it was all over and all I wanted to do was make it right with my girl.

Well now that wouldn't be so. I was on my way to the King County Jail. There, I would wait on Port Allen PD to come and pick me up. I knew the drill. I would go to court in the morning and the judge will ask what I'm doing in Seattle and that Port Allen PD has ten (10) days to come and get me. If they fail to do so they will let me go. Well I knew I wasn't going to be let go. They always come and get you. Now I'm back to having thirty (30) years hanging over my head. I can't think about Jeanne' at this time. I have to focus on me and at this point, my life is over. Thirty (30) years is a long time to be on a job. It's definitely a long time to be dead. Shit, any amount of time behind bars is too much for me to even think about but at the same time I felt relieved. Finally it's over. Now somehow I've got to fight. Shit this is my life we're talking about, thirty (30) years was like a life sentence to me.

Somehow I have to forget the past, just thinking about that day when I was busted — having all that dope right in front of me. There was no question in my mind at the time. It was an open and shut case. But somehow I have to muster up some hope and faith. In the last couple of years I've been around people of faith and I think I've learned enough to hold on to hope. While I was waiting for the Port Allen PD to come and get me there was something inside of me telling me, "It's not time to give up."

The thought of these thirty (30) years are weighing on my mind very heavily. I also find that I can't' leave Jeanne' hanging. I know right now she has no idea what's going on.

She hadn't come back home yet and by the time she finds out about this I should have come to the reality of all of this. Maybe by then I'll get a chance to try and explain the whole thing as best I can.

But where do I start? Here I was getting out of prison in California and on parole and I begged my parole officer to let me go to Louisiana. He really didn't want to because he felt it was a bad idea. I was determined though so he agreed and in a month's time I was in Louisiana with 2.2 lbs. of cocaine (Thank God my brother talked me out of taking the whole thing with me). After selling 2 ounces I got busted dead to rights. The case is open and shut. How the fuck do I explain that to her? Not only how do I explain but where is the hope in all this shit? I'm sorry and will you wait for me? Port Allen is known for throwing niggas away, especially if you don't have the money to hire an attorney. So how do I justify anything? I'm fucked. However, the thought of getting out of this and coming back to Seattle spending the rest of my life with my soul mate was a powerful thing. This became the motivating factor to come out of this situation. After a couple days of waiting for Port Allen PD to come I decided I had come up with a plan.

There's got to be something I could do. For starters the first thing I did was look for a bible. I went back in my mind and reflected on the pastor and what she said to me, about how God said not to worry and that thing I'm running from will be taken care of. At the time I was very freaked out because of her saying something like that especially since she didn't know my past at all, but for some reason when she said it I really did feel a sense of peace but I didn't understand it.

I grew up Baptist all I knew was "amen brother" and some shouting. It was normally the same people amening and shouting every Sunday. I didn't understand prophesy. So to have someone in front of me, a prophet and not only that but for them to prophesy about me was mind blowing. Although I ran away from that wonderful church, the experience I had there getting baptized and going through the whole Pentecostal experience was one I won't ever forget. I guess one of the reasons why I was able to last as long as I did and there's no better time to draw from that. Some might say here's another one of those cats the minute he goes to jail he calls on the Lord. Well! Maybe just maybe this is what it takes for me and some others to come to Christ, coming to a place of needing Him like never before. When you read the bible you read about all of these guys that God has bailed out of trouble, what's so different about me and them? At this point I have nothing but time anyway so why not call on the God I had as a boy when I was sad and alone. During that time in my life he so was real to me. Maybe God will remember me. It can't hurt to get down on my knees and call on Him.

There was nothing to do at that point but wait. I have nothing to lose but everything to gain. When I called on him in the Port Allen jail somehow I got out of that situation and that's how I got here (even though I did turn my back on him when I got here).

Well, maybe I'm still that little boy from Sunrise to God and He'll come to my aide once again (I did tell God that I didn't want to be a preacher, maybe He won't hold that against me). I'm just going to have to take this one day at a time. I mean I've always heard in church about forgiveness and the goodness of God. And besides, I think I know more about God now than I ever did before. I'll take what I've learned in that little church and go back to the Port Allen jail and cry out to God with no holding back. It's my life that on the line. I must remember that at every waking moment. Now that I have some understanding of faith and belief along with some direction, I feel I could go forward in a positive manner. I just have to remember that no matter what it looks like in Louisiana, I got to stay focused.

I have to try to get in touch with Jeanne'. To be able to talk to her before I leave would be so big to me. When we talk she may give me a sign of some kind. I've been here a few days and no sign of the Port Allen PD. Is this the hope preachers talk about? Another day and another day pass and still no Port Allen PD. Inside I'm ready to shout but I am a realist. On the ninth day the jailer came on the cell block to tell me that someone was here to see me. I'm all fucked up not knowing who, maybe its Jeanne' or maybe they are letting me go. Just imagine what was going on in my mind. They had ten (10) days to come and get me and being the ninth (9) day you just don't know what could happen. well that ninth day,I was taken from my cell,they said I was going to be interviewed.

When I got to the room it was my mother's cousin who was a detective in Port Allen, Lloyd Talbert. At that moment all hope of getting out of this situation was gone. I told myself to stay focused and show the police how confident I am about getting out of this situation. Lloyd Talbert and I talked about all kinds of things from what he thought will happen to Bill, concerning the conviction and to be honest he knew

everything concerning us and what we did, he knew about
our drug addiction. I must admit he warned me many
times, but just like everyone who was under the bondage
of drugs, I didn't listen. There were family members who
were very bitter towards Lloyd and me. This was due to
Bill's conviction. my aunts were very bitter because of it.
Personally I didn't think that was fair at all. When I said
something about that it was pushed aside and that made
me feel like an outsider sometimes. I guess, when you are
a mother, you don't want to face the fact that your kid has
gone wrong. So you call wrong right and right wrong.

While on the flight back we talked a lot and we had lots
of time, because we had a layover in Dallas. I sensed he
wanted me to hear him out and I was more than willing
to. I have never blamed anyone including the police for my
downfall. I knew what drugs and crime would do and where
it would lead. My eyes were wide open. So I didn't blame
Lloyd or any other cop for what I'm doing and I didn't want
my mom to do that either. Oh God! Lloyd shared so much
with me that day and after the plane ride I understood so
much of what was happening with Geraldine, Ruby and my
mom. As for my case, all he said was don't worry about it. It
will be o.k.

Wow! Talking to Lloyd was like déjà vu. I've heard this before. Right then I remembered what the pastor said that day while she was prophesying over me. After hearing that from him, that sealed the deal for me. That went deep in my spirit and in my mind I'm going to fight and somehow God was going to get me out of this. I was going back to the woman and the city where I think I belong. As Lloyd and I talked he said he had taken in a game or two of the Seattle baseball team and went to Pike Place market and some other attractions. The last thing he told me was that he had gone by the apartment where Jeanne' and I lived. He said it was a real nice, clean place. I think he met Jeanne' but he didn't say and I didn't ask. I really just want to get back and deal with this. Also, unlike other times when I was taken back to California those who came and got me humiliated me using hand cuffs and leg restraints. Maybe that was necessary in a normal situations but I was on crutches and at that time there was no way that I could have done anything. Lloyd found no reason to do anything of the sort. I felt good about myself going through the airport. I have so much respect for him doing that.

I'm back in the Port Allen jail and it hasn't changed that much but there's something missing. It took me a day or two to figure out what it was. It was Roebe. He had played a very important role leading up to this. I'm sure he had seen all kinds of guys coming in here on different charges but to him there was something about me. He and I played it for everything it was worth. He was the one who took me to the hospital in New Orleans and just left me there. It would have been nice if he had been here this time around, but it was not meant to be. You see Roebe passed away. Man! That guy and I went at it almost every day. When they told me he passed my heart went out to his family (it truly did).

My brother was in jail at this time and he was a cook. That was a good thing because a lot of the food I wouldn't eat. It was horrible my first time around and believe me it hadn't changed. Having my brother as one of the cooks meant I was getting hamburgers and etc. Whenever he was working and I don't think he stayed but a few months. After leaving the jail he went on to the penitentiary and that was the end of the burgers, etc.

Chapter 19

The LAW FIRM

It wasn't long before I received some hope. One of my brother's friends had come across this law firm. At the time they were making a name for themselves in the Baton Rouge and West Baton Rouge areas by handling most of the big drug cases, murder cases and whatever else with success. Word was going around about this law firm. Maybe this is the prophecy that my pastor had given me that night. I arranged for one of the law partners to come and see me. This law firm had handled my brother's case and one of his friends case also and many other guys I knew. These lawyer's had made a lot of money off of the dope boys. So I guess they were thinking I had the kind of money my brother and his friends had I got to meet with him and look at my options but I needed money. I knew I wasn't going to get money from anybody in my family, my mom, my cousins, and no one.

After going over my case with the lawyer and listening to him I felt good about him working on my case. I can't explain why, it just felt right. At the end of our meeting I asked him one question and I wanted total honesty. I asked, "What are the odds of me walking out of here with you as my lawyer? Be truthful." He looked me in my eyes and said, "eighty-five (85) percent." That did it for me. With no hesitation I said, "You have the job and I'll call you about the money in a day or two." Well I have a problem. Where do I get the money from? I knew if my Uncle Jay had been doing good it wouldn't be any question about the money, but he's been out of work for quite some time now. The only other person would be my Uncle Rozelle and I knew deep down inside he wouldn't let me down and with the help of my mother, it's no way he would say no.

I knew how much he loved my mom and from the beginning when I first went to San Francisco he showed me so much kindness. He never stopped showing kindness to me until this day. I couldn't wait to call him and tell him my situation. I had to call him at work. I didn't know how he would take that but that was the only option I had. I called and he was cool and also he was the boss. I explained to him what was going on and that I had talked to a lawyer. I explained that the lawyer was eighty-five (85) percent sure that I would walk out of here. The only thing he asked was if I believed the lawyer. I told him yes. He said ok he would pay.

I thanked God and got into my bible. In a day or two I called the lawyer and gave him my uncle's information. I was ready to go to war with the D.A. My uncle and the lawyer talked because not long after my meeting with him he was back to see me to tell me what his plan was. To be honest after retaining him as my lawyer I wasn't worried about my case anymore. I felt like this guy was going to fight for me. My job was to stay positive and make sure my uncle kept the checks coming in.

Everything seemed to be going well until I called my uncle one day. He said that two of his sisters (my aunts) — Geraldine and Ruby felt that he was wasting his money on me because they felt like I was going to prison no matter what. I could tell that he had been pondering this. I reassured him that the lawyer and I were more than confident that I would walk. He must have believed me because he continued to pay the lawyer. As for my aunts speaking against me, the only thing I could chalk that up to was either something from the past or something to do with Bill going to prison. As I recalled they felt it was my fault that he went to prison. Still holding on to that they wanted me to pay the price. Little did they know I paid a price and was still paying for my part? Yet and still I wasn't angry with them nor did I ever say anything.

My uncle was too smart to listen to them. He knew me
for himself. He knew the real me away from all of the
bullshit. My mom's sister Betty knew me too, but for some
reason she refused to say anything to Ruby and Geraldine.
I couldn't worry about my family right now, my main
concern had to be helping the lawyer with my case. This
was serious.

While in this place I was laid back. I pretty much kept to
myself, just reading my Bible and maintaining my focus. At
some point Jeanne' and I started communicating again. I
was overjoyed. The first thing she wanted me to know was
that she still loved me. Secondly, she wanted to know how
long I will be gone and thirdly if I was coming back. There
was no question I loved her as well. As for how long I would
be gone, though I was confident I would get off easy, I just
couldn't give her an answer. If everything went the way I
wanted of course I was going back.

At this point I had to explain to her what I was charged
with and the kind of time I was facing. I also had to tell
her about my background, and it wasn't good at all. After
hearing this, I'm sure it would be hard for someone to wait
on me especially with the odds stacked against me. We
tried our best to be honest with each other at least that

was my intention. She made me feel like she was willing to stand by me as long as I believed in my chances. I did everything I could to reassure her. I told her that my lawyer also believed I would walk. I even had the lawyer call her at times. Still it must have been tough on her finding out this way. Shit! Thirty (30) years man! That's a lot. How could someone ask a woman to deal with that?

I knew I couldn't ask her to wait on me, I wouldn't do it. If this was the other way around I knew I wouldn't wait, so I couldn't ask her to carry that burden. It seemed impossible for me to bear, but I had no choice in the matter. When it was all said and done, I felt like I had done enough to give our future a small chance. What I mean is six (6) months wouldn't be too much before she should move on. I didn't say this to her, I didn't have the right, because she wasn't my wife. I just kept this thought to myself. I felt I brought a lot to the table and with that in mind I let the chips fall where they may. At the end of the day it's about the charges I'm facing. And come to think of it, I don't know who told my mom thirty (30) years. Since I've been back in jail with the same charges plus an escape charge added to it I haven't heard one word about thirty (30) years. Actually I haven't heard anything at all about my future.

One day while I was meeting with my lawyer I asked if the D.A. had come to him with any kind of deal. He assured me that he was taking nothing less than me walking out of the door. As he gave me hope I would pass it on to Jeanne'. This would seem to fill her with joy. Sometimes it felt as though I was selling her false dreams. The weeks had turned into months and to be honest at times I felt like my lawyer was selling me false hope. At this time all I heard from my lawyer was basically, "Show me the money." He never said anything negative to me but I knew the money was a driving force for him.

I reminded myself I had to trust God. There had been too many instances already when God had come through. No I wasn't walking with the Lord but I wasn't crazy either. I knew that something divine was working on my behalf. I mean the first time I was here and the prophetess told me to read those chapters in the book of Psalms every day and I would walk out of this jail. Ok so it wasn't a clean break but just like she said I did walk out of here. There has been too much evidence of Jesus' divine intervention that I just couldn't overlook it. Knowing this I still never considered being saved. I just didn't see God that way.

Even though I would call on him and I've always gotten the answer I wanted I still couldn't or wouldn't come to Him as I should've. Maybe I didn't want religion and I didn't know the person of Jesus. It seemed like church people made it look so distant. Besides I'm so street and I wanted things my way with no boundary. Maybe it wasn't church folks, maybe I just wanted what I wanted. Who knows!?

If I come out of this maybe I'll go back to church but all of that was going to have to wait. My lawyer is coming to see me more and more at this point to talk about the case. He's pretty confident about the outcome and he had not been this confident in the past. Don't get me wrong I like this attitude, but let me in on what's going on. Well, apparently he went to law school with the judge's clerk and though he didn't go into detail he was working on something, maybe some sort of deal that would allow me to walk out of here. Needless to say it's been months since I've been here and this is the best news I've had so far. I could hardly wait to talk to Jeanne' to tell her. He didn't say I was.

When I talked to Jeanne' I tried to be cool but I could tell the months were weighing on her and she needed to be lifted up. I knew it was hard on her with all the bills. It was all on her the car note, everything. Just maybe this was the news she needed to hear. I tried my best not to read too much into what the lawyer said but I will admit I was filled with hope and I wanted her to believe in me. I can truly say everything was good between us at this time. I guess that old saying is true - "You can't run from your past, it'll catch up with you eventually." Well even that being the case the news about my case seemed to make her happy. On the surface she seemed to be happy for me but I'm no fool. I'll just wait until I walk out of this jail. Then and only then will everything be real to me. I know I have some trust issues, after all look how we started. I mean I was with another woman and she knew this, but I wanted to believe she would wait for me.

I had to look at the facts though. Look at how I was willing to end it, not willing to talk about what I was going through and trying to push it aside and live with it. It eventually got the best of me. Would she or could she ever see this my way? I must not let it weigh me down because if buying the car and putting her in a nice place didn't show her how much I loved her nothing else will. In the meantime my lawyer and I had been doing great on my case.

The thing that stood out the most was the fact he asked for my input and he shared all his information with me.

Together we were putting together a very good defense and this went on for some months and finally I got a court date and leading up to that day my wife had filed for divorce and the sheriff came to my cell and served me the papers. Because of the case and the seriousness of my charge I could care less, fuck! I'm facing thirty (30) years. As far as I was concerned she didn't exist, plus I was in love with Jeanne'.

As you could imagine the night before my court date I couldn't sleep. After running from this for a few years it all came down to this and 9:00 a.m. had passed and I'm still sitting in my cell, man! They were calling guys out to go to court, but no Herbert. It's still early maybe my lawyer got caught in traffic. I'm nervous and I'm ready to get this started and over. Now everyone had been to court. It's 3:00 p.m. and from experience I know I'm not going to court today. The question is why?

Around dinner time the jailer came around to my cell to tell me to call my lawyer. This cant' be good. He takes me to the phone and before I could say anything he assures me that everything is all good. The issue is that my uncle hadn't sent the check for my last payment. Shit! That scared the hell out of me. I said ok, don't worry I'll call him and see what the problem is. Man! This lawyer fucker thinks he is slick. He postponed the court date so he could get paid. It took me a couple of days to get in touch with my uncle. I called his office and his secretary said he has been busy. On the inside of me I'm saying don't quit now Uncle. It's the last payment. I could feel it man! I'm out of here just send him the check. I finally get to talk to my uncle and maybe he was having some doubts and I could understand that but this is it. I had to reassure him once again that everything is cool and pay this guy. This should be the last one. He felt good about that. I guess him hearing the confidence in my voice made him realize my lawyer and I believe in my chances. In a day or two my lawyer had received the money and he was ready to go back to court.

There are going to be a lot of sleepless nights as far as I was concern and knowing that I did everything I could to help my case, made me sleep a little easier this time around. There's one more thing I have to do and it's going to be hard and that's telling Jeanne' the court date has been pushed back another thirty (30) days or so. When I told her what happened she seemed to be ok with it, but at this point I don't think she believes that I'm getting out of here. I had to explain to her it was just about the money and not the case itself. I also let her know my lawyer and I talked to my uncle and he's going to pay what should be the last payment. She said she was ok but I couldn't tell if she really was or not. I couldn't worry about that not now. No question, I wanted her to believe but most importantly I had to believe for myself. Man! It's my freedom on the line. I had to focus.

My court date is finally here again! Just like with the first court date I couldn't sleep the night before. This time it's happening and when they started calling names mine was first. I found out when I got downstairs in the court room that this was some kind of motion. It was to see if there was enough evidence to bring it to court or to dismiss the case. My lawyer was looking forward to this. Since I had escaped and been gone a few years he thought that the police should have a problem remembering the things that might be important to the D.A.'s case and that would be an advantage to my defense. To me that made perfect sense. This could force the judge and the D.A. to throw the case out of court, but that's not likely just because of my criminal history.

Well just as my lawyer thought they couldn't remember a lot of important information that was vital to the D.A.'s case. Bargaining with me wasn't a bad idea for the D.A. but after all this is Port Allen and these fuckers don't have a problem railroading your ass at all. At the end of the day my lawyer was very confident in our chances of walking out of here the next time we came to court. Knowing the system like I do now, I knew that was just about a ninety (90) day process from start to finish barring no setbacks. It was set back once and that was my lawyer's doing but now he's paid. I knew one thing for sure and that's within sixty days I would be walking out of here or taking that ride to Hunt's prison.

I made sure I read my Bible in the morning and in the evening. It wasn't just because of the case either. Somehow I found that reading the Bible brought me a peace I couldn't get by myself. Even though on the streets I thought I was smart enough to do it myself. As in the past I would end up being my own worst enemy. When I'm in jail or in trouble I would pick up the Bible and turn to God. Somehow, someway I would get the answer I was seeking but yet I still wouldn't walk with Him as I did as a boy. Even back then I only called on Him when I was sad or hurt by something. He always made it better. I remember as a nine (9) year old kid I said to God, "I don't want to be no preacher." I said all this to say that, as my next court date approaches in my heart I knew I would be walking out of here. Besides I couldn't afford to think no other way.

The night before court I couldn't sleep. I must have read my Bible all night and in the morning I must have gotten dressed for 7:00 a.m. Court didn't start until 9:00 a.m. but I was just ready to face it and get it over with. To my surprise my lawyer came to the cell. At first I was like (what the fuck). He said, "Hey listen to me, here's the deal, you can take probation and walk out of here today and also they are going to let you go back to Seattle, by transferring your probation there. " There is no question I am taking that, but "What about my parole in California?" I ask. He said not to worry about that now. We needed to take care of this first and then we would look into the parole in California. To be honest getting from under these thirty (30) years was first and foremost. I felt like the whole world has been lifted off of my shoulders. After giving it some more thought — California, I could care less! I'll just let the lawyer handle this, thinking he has worked out a deal with California to run my parole concurrent with the probation I'm getting in Louisiana, but hey, nobody talked about California. So I'm thinking they dropped the parole.

I just wanted to get out and go back to Seattle. I just didn't know. I was confused honestly and deep down inside of me I didn't want to know. I wanted to believe that my lawyer and the D.A. had worked all of this out. Besides, there was no way they was going to let me go knowing I was on parole in California. In fact when I got busted I had only been out of prison thirty (30) days. So in my mind they had to know this and I'll just leave it in their hands. It's not my job to tell them anything.

Chapter 20

Seattle, Jeanne'...Here I Come Again

After agreeing to my plea, my lawyer went back to the D.A. and about an hour later I was brought downstairs to the court room to hear my charges and accept the deal. I didn't bring up California and the only thing on my mind is getting back to Seattle and Jeanne'. This time it's going to be different. I'll be in a city that I have come to love and I'll have the type of woman I've always wanted — (my soul mate). Man! I couldn't get back soon enough. It would be a few days though. I have to wait on the probation department to do whatever it is that they do. When it is time to go and get the paper work from the probation department I go see the probation officer and they arrest me right then and there. I'm like (oh shit)! The first thing that comes to mind is the parole back in California, but why did they let me get this far. I kept my cool and called my lawyer. He said he didn't know anything about this. To his credit he got to the jail right away. After spending the night in jail I was told having been on parole, I didn't qualify for probation on these type of charges. But luckily I along with the judge, the D.A. and my lawyer, I had already signed the probation papers and they couldn't be voided.

I got out of jail the next morning and a few days later I got my transfer papers to Seattle. It wasn't soon enough for me. I could hardly wait to see Jeanne'. I loved my mother but spending a day or two was all I could take. I got to go. Finally I could be myself, but I knew it would be bittersweet.

In the beginning after my escape I met a lot of good people and I lied to them. While I was in jail I felt that if I was to get out the thing to do was to go to everyone and tell them the truth. I honestly wanted to do that. The first place I wanted to go was that little Pentecostal church that embraced me and filled me with hope and even offered me a place to stay. Man! I can't forget the love the pastor and everybody else in the church showed me. It was amazing. At the time the guilt and shame along with facing thirty (30) years stopped me from being honest with people who seemed to genuinely care about me. I walked away from the only thing that was real in my life. I wanted to go by the car wash too and say hi to Rob and try to tell him the truth as well. After all he had done so much for me when I first came to Seattle. The car wash is where I met those church folk.

It will be much easier to talk to Rob than to the church. Maybe I was still just too ashamed to face the church. Lying to Rob was one thing but lying to God's people and turning my back on God was another. I'll have to think long and hard about this. In the meantime Jeanne' and I are ready to do this again. She hasn't once brought up the past and I'm relieved.

I said some things that I wish I could have taken back. I wanted to tell her what was going on in my head but she insisted that it was in the past and to just come home. She said that she had a job driving a recycle truck for Harley whom I also know and by the time I get back Harley would have a contract in Portland with a recycle company. She let me know she had my back until I could get back on my feet. I've always been the one to carry my family financially so this would be a little different, but it is what it is. There was no place for foolish pride and I have to rid myself of my pride if I wanted my soul mate. I knew it wouldn't be long before I was back on my feet.

When I got back to Seattle it was just as she said. The passion between us was still there as it was in the very beginning of our relationship. It was just like I dreamed it would be. It was all good except... she had a dent on the passenger side door of the car. It wasn't bad but still if I buy something for you take care of it. That's no small thing by any means. That's the second biggest investment you can make after a home. Well, I can't sweat the small stuff. The boys were happy to see me and Sherika was ok with my return I guess. It was hard to tell. After all I had said some things to her mother before I was taken to jail that were totally out of order. Sherika was fourteen (14) she knew I was good before I started tripping. She and I were close but still I said some stupid shit in front of her. She not knowing what I was going through was hurt by the things I said and the way I treated her mother while saying them. In her eyes I was just like Jeanne's husband — verbally abusive. Thank God the boys were still too young to understand. I just needed and wanted to earn back sherika trust.

I thought maybe telling her my story would be the thing to bring us back to where we used to be. But I knew it was going to take some time regardless of what I said or did. Right now I could feel and see the anger in her eyes. In spite of the way Sherika was acting, Jeanne' and I along with the boys were getting on with our life. We were trying to get back to some sense of normalcy. There were lots of lies on my part but my love for her and the kids was far from one of them. Everything now hinged on trust and it all starts with me. I was the one who had broken that bond of trust. Though she may know the truth, it's still going to take time for us to be one again.

Our lives were starting to take a turn for the better due to Harley's telling us that the job in Portland would be happening real soon. This was the thing we needed. I loved Seattle, but the move to Portland seemed to be the remedy that I so much needed. Plus, Harley promised me a position with the company in Portland. Man! Everything was falling into place. Jeanne' and Larry were going down to Portland to build the company up. This was a great opportunity for the both of them as well as me. Harley needed to see if I would have a problem with my girl being out front. It was me he had in mind for the job but I went to jail and with no one knowing if or when I would be getting out they offered the job to Jeanne'.

Jeanne' and I as well as Larry and his girl were invited to dinner to go over the details and to make sure everyone was on the same page. Wow! I'd only been back a short time and it couldn't get any better than this. Just the other day I was thinking my girl is the breadwinner and this is new to me. I've always had the money in the relationships and here I am about to start on a job at a new recycle center and be part of the process to build the center from the ground up. The way Harley explained it to me the building isn't complete nor is it in full operation at this point. This division of the recycle center that Harley is operating wouldn't be in full operation for at least six (6) months to a year. Larry and Jeanne' would be there to oversee Harley's division until completion and then I would be hired. I could possibly be hired before that. I just needed to be patient. Before the meeting I thought I would be going straight to work once we moved to Portland. This wasn't the case. After a few drinks my pride gave way to common sense and everything is cool with me. I'm ready for the move.

After being back for a few weeks, Sherika is still acting out a little. I'm not sure if it's because she doesn't want to go to Portland or if it was me. I was being a little tough on them about keeping their rooms clean. I'm trying to work on my relationships with the kids and be a better man for them as well as their mother. I'm also starting to move around the city a little bit more. It felt good moving around but I didn't like that car door being fucked up, but I would still clean the car up and roll out. Things are ok at least I thought so until one day Jeanne' comes home from work and she wasn't her happy about life smiling self.

I asked her what was wrong and obviously whatever it is she feels she has to tell me. She starts by telling me how much she loves me and does not want to lose me. Well after what I've just been through I just knew I could handle just about anything. She then said she wanted to be the first to tell me before I would hear it from someone else. I then asked, "What is it? Tell me." She said it only happened one time and that was it. I said, "Come on you have to tell me more than that." She then said that Harley put William on the truck with her for a week or two. One Friday after work they had some drinks together and they slept together that night. Well, I wasn't as strong as I thought and I wasn't as forgiving as she either. I had thought long and hard about something like this when I was in jail. I decided that I deserved at least six (6) months before she had gone out and fucked someone else.

It didn't help that I have been drinking that day. I lost it. I called her everything but a child of God. She cried and said how sorry she was and that she thought she would never see me again. What pissed me off was the fact that I knew William. He worked with us at the recycle center. The nigga was the kind of cat who got a kick out of fucking over you. He was one who was always listening to me about my dealings with my chicks. He jocked me back when I first started at the recycle center. I never hung out with him and as far as what happened with him and Jeanne' I didn't blame him. Man! I tried my best to understand and we made it through the night. I made love to her thinking it would change the way I feel and having this great opportunity in Portland. At this point I want out of Seattle, my pride is hurt but it didn't hit me until I was by myself. Not only that, when I thought about it I'm thinking she should not have done this shit.

Now my imagination is running wild. I'm asking myself how many niggas has it been. I had to ask her has it been others. She assured me that it was nobody else and I so wanted to believe her but I have a problem with bitches who do that, always have. After knowing this (I still love her) and all I could think of was let me get past this. I'm a grown ass man, besides look at what I did to Yolanda and others I've been with payback is a motherfucker. I could get past this.

Hey I could do this and it's no better time to start than right now. So when she came home from work, I had dinner ready and (not only that) her bath water was ready also. This is what I did when we started this love affair and to my surprise it was just the thing we needed. However, there was a storm brewing inside of me and I didn't like that feeling at all and for the most part I suppressed it. I was good at doing that. Look at how long I held on to my last episode.

I've been forgiven many times by chicks I've hurt and maybe it's my time to forgive. My first test of forgiving will be at my favorite night club Hollywood Underground. Jeanne' and I had never been there together. Matter of fact this would be our first night out together since I've been back. For some reason I had gotten some powder cocaine from my buddy Tubby Cain and my intention was to enjoy my girl and show her a good time. But too many coke lines and drinks was beginning to bring out all that rage that I had held inside. She did nothing to bring this out either. The higher I got the more I looked at her and the more I thought about that nigga laying with my girl. At the same time putting down those drinks didn't help. She became all kinds of bitches and hoes and to make matters worse it was all going down on the dance floor.

What seemed to piss me off the most was how she handled it. She did absolutely nothing but be a lady. Out of the blue she grabbed me by the hand and began to pull me out of the club. I guess I wanted to shame her in front of everybody in the club. By no means did I feel good about what I did in the club, but I wanted her to know how she had hurt me. I must admit she was a strong chick to let me go off on her and not say a word until I had let it all out. Then all she said was get it all out of your system and let's be done with this and go back in the club and dance and then go home and love each other. But no, not me! I took that as that bitch getting the best of me and out of the blue I slapped her ass and then I was seeing stars, this bitch had hit me with her purse and the next thing I knew she was out of the high hills and running. In a drunken rage I began to run after her.

There was no way I was catching her. I was too drunk and high and at that moment I needed to get myself together. It wasn't long before she came back and I began to apologize right away so we laugh it off and went back in the club as though nothing had happened. Somehow I kept my disappointment and bitterness under wraps and if ever I needed to grow up and become a man it was now. I knew in my heart I still loved this girl and everybody makes mistakes. I've made my share of course and besides who am I to judge her.

For the most part I continued on in love and peace knowing that we were moving to Portland. If I could just get this bullshit out of my mind and focus on our future together.

Well, I felt we were getting past this and then the time came for Jeanne' and Larry to go down to Portland with their boss on business. They began to do this quite often. This showed me not only was I hurt by the William thing, but now I have a serious trust issue.

When Jeanne' was in Portland I would drink often and think about who she's with and what she's doing the whole time she's gone. I'm cool when she comes back, but I'm really hurting inside and I don't know how to handle this. I really want to forgive and forget and give her another chance. Hey! I was just given a second chance. Just looking back a few months ago I was facing thirty (30) years in a Louisiana prison and yet I've been given another chance. I've done a lot of bullshit to women in the past. So what gives me the right to be mad with her? I'm all fucked up over this, so what? I got fucked over, the old saying says, "What goes around comes around." Now the right thing to do was leave this in the past.

Many times it may have been hard for her to talk about this but I would make her listen to my point of view and try to convince her that I will change my attitude and enjoy this second chance I have with her. As I look into her eyes I could see that she wanted so much to believe me but the

question is do I believe me? To be honest I didn't know
what to do. When she was in Portland with Harley and
Larry, my mind was running wild with all kinds of bullshit.
When she's down there I'm tripping. For one thing drinking
that Old English 800 Malt Liquor and chasing it with Brandy
and (man) it wasn't helping this situation at all, but it's been
my comfort zone for as long as I can remember and it was
the thing I've always turned to.

At this point I kept my feelings to myself. There were a
few times when she was in Portland I would call her late
not wanting much just to talk. She would handle it with
such grace. The next day I would feel so stupid. When
she thought I was up she would call and tell me about the
meeting and what they were doing that day. The situation
was starting to take a toll on me and it was no question I
was making it hard for her as well.

Clearly I wasn't the same man she met a year or so ago. I
so needed to be that man again. I had fought so hard to get
back here to her and now I can't seem to get past one night
she had with this guy. It seems I'm going to go off on the
deep end if I don't get my shit together I could lose her and
maybe this time for good. If I keep drinking this cheap ass
liquor I know I'll lose her because drinking would make

me push her away. I have to dig deep down inside of what seems to be a shell of a man and find a way to move past the storm I'm in. The problem is when she's gone away I can't trust her and when she's here with me I can't stand to look at her. Sometimes, many times actually I am asking myself why I am here. I'm not happy with her but then again I'm not happy without her. I guess I'm caught between a rock and a hard place.

Right now there is nothing I could do about it. She's happy as could be apparently I'm back and she's about to start a new job in a new city. Pretty soon I'll be on board and in reality I should be just as happy and right now no matter how I feel I just can't burst her bubble and at this point I'm really trying my best not to.

It's time to pack up and move to Portland. As of now the kids are going to stay in Seattle with their dad. Sherika's arrangements with her father are not final so for the time being she'll stay with Jeanne's dad. Sherika didn't seem happy about the idea of moving. Still not sure if it was me or just leaving Seattle. In the meantime she felt she should drop one last bomb. She decided to tell me what was going on while I was in jail in Louisiana. Well what could she say that was any worse than the things that had already been said by Jeanne'?

I have to give it to Sherika. I always knew she was a clever girl, but she caught me totally by surprise with this one. She waited until I was drunk and she asked me to come into the room to talk. I knew she didn't want to move to Portland and I thought that's what she wanted to talk about but she had a different look in her eyes. I sobered up a little bit because I sensed it was more than just moving to Portland. We sat down to talk and to my surprise she said that not only had her mom slept with William but with Larry too. Oh my God! My whole world came crashing down on me. Again!

I was already fucked up and now Sherika has hit me with this. I don't think I could ride this out. My first thought was could this be true and Sherika knowing how much it would hurt me she couldn't be this mean unless it's true. Ok! I'm trying to keep my composure in front of her. I'm trying not to let her see the hurt and pain her words have caused me. So I lied and said it's ok. I wasn't here when this was going on and she didn't know if I was coming back and that's understandable considering the situation at that time, but Sherika was pushing all the right buttons.

She was saying she thought I had a right to know. On the inside I was in a rage. My mind is running about a hundred miles an hour. Thank God Jeanne' wasn't here, but then again maybe if she was it would end here and now, but by her being away I have time to plot and boy the anger was building and I'm at the point of no return. Just that quick I am thinking about revenge. I have to be smart about this. What if Sherika is just being mean and wants me to blow up and leave. I have a chance to forgive and have the life that I want so much so I have to be very careful about how I approach this. To top things off I have to ask about Larry and be in control of my emotions at the same time.

Could it just be Sherika starting shit? Man! We are already dealing with this William thing and I don't need to get all fucked up about something that may not be true and most importantly I need to be sober. When she got home I was cool but I was on edge and I just wanted to get to the point. That's not the way I needed to deal with this. I wanted to treat it like a rumor but being pissed off wasn't going to get me anywhere I knew that from the past.

I've learned that the only way to deal with Jeanne' is to be up front because that's how she deals with people; that's how we were when we got together and somehow I need

to get back to that person I was back then. Maybe I could
see clearly the road I should take if I could get back to that
person. Will I or better yet can I get back to that person?
I know that's what I want, but it seems that I'm so full of
selfish pride thinking about what someone else is thinking
about me.

I don't know where this kind of thinking is coming from
because I've never worried about what people thought of
me. If this is love and I feel and act this way I don't want this
because I feel like I'm weak and she's in control. Then again
I feel she loves me, because she in the past left everything
she knew to be with me and I did the same. We know that
what we have is real. Her husband was a real asshole he
made a lot more money than I did yet she chose to be with
me. Her not knowing if I would leave Yolanda, yet she was
willing to risk her marriage and leaving her kids to be with
me. If I find out she slept with Larry I don't know what
I'll do. When she got home from work, I tried to wait for
a better time because Sherika was home and we had just
finished talking about this. I was sure Jeanne' didn't have a
clue as to what Sherkia told me.

Right then and there I should have backed off and gave this
a lot of thought. Right then it felt like a lie but I was too far

gone. I asked her about Larry sleeping in my bed and first she seemed shocked about the question. Before she could say a word I started screaming at the top of my voice and as always she was calm and trying to calm me down. She was asking me the question — "Who said that?" I was trying my best not to bring Sherika into this but I finally told her, "Your daughter." She instantly began focusing on Sherika and she began to ask her why she lied to me. For a moment I didn't know what to believe. She went at Sherika real hard. Well I know Jeanne' well enough to know when she's pissed and right now she's pissed. I wasn't helping matters because while she was chewing out Sherika's ass, I was chewing her ass out. No one got any rest that night.

I really wanted to believe Jeanne' but I asked myself why would her daughter lie on her like that? She knew I would confront her mother and not only that but to lie like this she must really hate her mother or me. It didn't matter what Jeanne' said Sherika stuck to her story. And from that night on I really wanted Sherika to say it wasn't true but she never did. Now I'm walking around like a ticking time bomb just waiting to explode. It became a game of who can hurt who the most at least that's how I saw it. I had become the master of hurting people and now since I couldn't get six months of her waiting for me before she slept with someone I feel she didn't love me. I understand she didn't know but if you cared at all six months should have been doable. Day by day my love was turning to hate and I began to think about how to get even. For one thing I wanted everybody that knew us to know that she fucked William and I'm angry as hell.

Still I wanted to make this relationship work. Deep down in my heart that's what I needed and now this. I got to deal with the thought of her sleeping with Larry. You see, William and I weren't that close but Larry that was a different story. He and I had developed a relationship before Jeanne' came along and when Fat Cat had come out here, Larry and Fat Cat really became good friends. I mean! They both had this love for weed and this nigga would be over to my apartment all the time. The thought of him sleeping with my girl hit me hard. The fact that he'll be in Portland was going to be a hard pill to swallow but somehow I got to do it. If this rumor turns out to be true, I wanted him to see me mentally abuse this bitch. At the same time if it's a total lie I have to deal with that too. As I said before I'm too far gone and so filled with anger.

The truth and the lie feels the same. Ok, I guess I'm just confused at this point. For one thing there's absolutely no trust on my part. Still I'm holding on to her somehow. It's not my nature to quit even if it's for all the wrong reasons. Now the only thing to do is to wait and see. Just maybe things will be different in Portland. Also there's a chance that Jeanne' will go to Larry with this and he'll come to me and say it's a lie and that he'll never do anything like this to me. Hey! It could happen but also I got to deal with what's eating me. Right about now alcohol and anger have taken a toll on my mind and it seems one day I love her and the next day I hate her. Fuck! I got to get myself together before I go crazy or maybe I'm already crazy. Well, it's getting closer and closer for our big move to Portland and I've managed to stay focused on our relationship as a couple. I'll admit this! I love her and when I look at her I don't see this person I so want to hurt.

In spite of the way I'm acting at times, she loves me the same way she did at the beginning. Of course I only saw the way she loves me when I'm sober. Being sober would be the answer to all my problems. No drinking, no problem! That's easier said than done. Before all of this, just like any other guy, when the games are on I enjoy having a drink or two, hanging out with my boys, drinking was something we do. After this drinking was different once I had that first drink the anger and bitterness would come over me. I didn't know what the truth was or what a lie was. Now the question is do I want this kind of life with this girl, or do I want her to be just as I am and we know what that is bitter, angry and hateful. I know in my heart no one deserves to be hurt. I'm cool for now.

One Saturday Harley and his wife invited Jeanne' and I along with Larry and his girlfriend over to their house for a little get together before we leave. I know I could get through this I must stay focused because this is a good test to see what's really inside of me. It wouldn't be that long before one too many drinks would reveal how I'm feeling on the inside. I hadn't seen Larry in almost a whole year or more yet, I had almost nothing to say and I don't think Jeanne' had said anything about what Sherika had said to me. Lord knows I wanted to confront him but I wasn't 100% sure it was true. Besides he had no idea what I was thinking. Also, I needed to deal with the fact that I had become friends with so many people that I felt cared a lot about me and yet I didn't tell them about my past. So before I have my pity party I must man up and talk about why I didn't tell the very people who trusted me in their lives, allowing me into their homes, etc. You would think it would be easy at this point but when I look around at these people who had given so much of themselves to me, I still found it very hard to be open.

Yes I am free from the case and the law, but I still found it hard to say I'm sorry for hiding my past from them. Instead I found it easier to be angry and bitter for what Jeanne' did with dude and now maybe Larry. This side of me would soon raise its ugly head. And as always the case of me doing the right thing would have to wait. Before I knew it I was drunk and very rude. I have always flirted with Harley's wife, Barbara and they have always just laughed it off. But I'm a different person right now. The way I treated Jeanne', I became so cold to her and to them it must have been somewhat shocking. They knew how much I loved her in the past and in my mind I thought that everybody knew about her and William and I wanted everybody to know that this bitch isn't getting away with this.

It was obvious I was heading down the wrong road here. As always Jeanne was the bigger person and as always she didn't go there with me at all. It must have been obvious that I was troubled by something and at this point everyone had pretty much ignored me for the rest of the evening and refused to listen to me about anything negative about Jeanne'. So I just continue to drink the night away and maybe that was the best thing. I paid for it the next day not only was I hung over, but I also felt ashamed about the way I treated Jeanne' in front of everyone. Instead of saying I was sorry I made it seem like it was her fault that I was this way. Unlike me she went out and did something to make it better. She went and brought something she knew I would like and made us a beautiful dinner. She did whatever she could to put this behind us. She went out of her way to try and fix me as best she could.

I was finding it hard to move on for some reason. The question for me now is how do I come at Larry with this and not look like a sucker. On the other hand I have to stay sober. Right now I don't know how much damage I did to my chance of getting that job Harley had promised me. Fucking with Jeanne' and Larry right now is not the chance I need to take so I need to pull myself together and at least act like everything is going to be alright and who knows maybe it will. Well, right now the most important thing is to stay sober and make this move to Portland. Maybe start over with Jeanne'. I'm fighting to be a man about this and… the question is am I going to let this foolish pride take me down, but damn there's a war going on inside of me and I don't have anyone outside of the woman in my life at the time to talk to.

I had never opened up to any of the guys I've been friends with. It seems like from birth I've been a loner and in spite of the highs and lows I would not shed a tear. I would just pull myself up somehow and keep going and this would be no different.

Chapter 21

Portland It's All About ME

It's moving day and I'm ready and willing to give this
relationship some kind of chance, I mean after all it cost
my uncle a lot of money to get me here. I have probation
to deal with and needless to say I still have her, but will
that be enough for me. Jeanne', Larry and Harley had come
down a month ago and got the apartment and it was a nice
place. Of course Larry and his girlfriend were moving in the
same building. Of course that was going to be a challenge
for me and it's no better time to be sober than now. In the
beginning she was working long hours and I made her feel
comfortable when she got home. I knew she would miss
the kids and I stayed sober trying to help her make that
transition.

I was used to moving around and meeting new people.
Wow! I surprised myself to how good I was doing in
Portland. I stayed away from Larry as much as possible
without him noticing how different I was being around
him. That was one of the reasons I was doing so good. Not
working I felt like a little bitch waiting on Jeanne' to give

me money. Don't get me wrong she was wonderful, but I needed a job. She wanted me to wait for Harley but for some reason I had become somewhat angry with Harley. For what reason I don't know. Maybe I felt he knew what happened between Jeanne' and William or maybe even Larry for all I know. That's just the way I saw it.

I don't know anything about the city and it was obvious I needed to get a newspaper. There were lots of jobs for welders, truck drivers, etc. I had no skills at all, but there was this one ad that got my attention. It said something about being your own boss and must have reliable transportation and have good communication skills. Shit! I thought I've sold dope for a living and had to deal with all kinds of bullshit, and I had a car. So I called and I was told to come down to the warehouse, without having much information about the job, I was all in. Now I can take my rightful place in this house. I could hardly wait until Jeanne' came home to tell her the good news though I didn't know anything about the job all I knew was I was going to make it work. After all the bullshit I was going through in Seattle, didn't seem to be important anymore and now I want to make this work with Jeanne'. After all she's here for me and she's doing everything she could to get me to put the past behind me. So why not give it a second chance whatever it takes. This is my mind set now, new city and new soon to be job. It doesn't get any better than this and being able to start over was one of the things I prayed for, and now it's here. The next day couldn't come soon enough.

I must have gotten up at about 4:00a.m. and I'll be honest I was nervous when I got there. I'm sitting waiting to see what my job will be because in the paper they didn't give much information and as I'm looking around in the warehouse all I see is boxes and more boxes. It's about ten other people besides myself. Finally some guy came out of an office and began to introduce himself to us who were there for the first time. He began to explain to us what the job is about and he goes over to one of the boxes and brings it and places it in front of all of us. He tells us to get in a circle and he opened up the box and pulls out a cookbook. He begins to explain to us how the system works. He said you are a sales person and you are your own boss. He said that they would supply us with the books and we could take as many as we wanted. That was it. They weren't just limited to books we would be selling all sorts of different things.

I must admit it wasn't what I envisioned for myself. I'm here now and the question is how much money is to be made and if I'm not mistaken it has something to do with a 60/40 split. I felt a little better because they had guys who had been doing this for a while, talking to us about what kind of money they were making. The guy in charge took us in a room and there was a big ass map of the Portland area hanging on the wall. He gave each one of us an area to work. How hard can it be? They give you the books, etc. They give you an area to work. That's not hard or is it? Well, now I got to go and tell Jeanne' because it's no weekly check. What I make will depend on me and only me. I knew she would support me but to be honest I don't know anything about Portland and the surrounding area, and also there's no guarantee of a weekly check. Not only that it's going to be wear and tear on the car. If you want to make money you're gonna have to load your car with books.

I didn't mind that as long as I would make money. I was willing to give it a chance. I'm not saying that this was life or death, but I didn't want to fail, not now. I was getting over something that's been holding me back — like William & Larry. I really wanted to move forward with this job.

On my first day everywhere I went people brought a book. I asked myself, "Is this real?" Maybe because it was cookbooks, I don't know, but I was excited. That first week went fast, but it was downhill from there. Maybe Portland wasn't big enough for the number of people we had roaming around. I did everything right I thought. I went to every little business in my area, but it seems like those cookbooks got old quick. We were promised more items but it was taking so long for them to arrive. We were only in week two. By week three I was just spinning my wheels and to make matters worse Jeanne' was pissed. There was no money coming in and I was wearing down our car. I couldn't blame her for being pissed.

In my mind I felt like as long as I was working I was contributing. The reality was I was only fooling myself. I was going nowhere. Jeanne' was very supportive but in week three she asked me to give the job up and I did. It was so hard to watch Larry take care of his family. I felt like the odd man out. At times my frustration would show but I played it cool because I didn't want to give Larry the satisfaction of watching me self-destruct. I was cool as long as I didn't think about the last twelve (12) months. I was disappointed that the job didn't work out but hey I did my best and that's all I could do.

I continued to look for work. One day while dropping Jeanne' off at work to my surprise I saw Joe. He was the guy who built the recycle center in Seattle where I worked. Though the center had been in operation for a while before I got there, Joe was still there making sure that everything went ok. At some point he came down to Portland to build one here. It was about thirty (30) percent completed. When I saw him the first thing that came to mind was to ask him for a job.

What do I have to lose? If he says yes I gain and if no I'll ask again. He said yes but not yet. After about two weeks of waiting and asking him when I thought about what I did in Seattle at the recycle center when I wanted the job there. I thought about how after asking Dick for a job for weeks I just decided to go buy some work boots and showed up one day to work. I told the foreman that Dick said to put me to work. It worked in Seattle so I figured it just might work here.

One morning I got up and dressed for work and walked in and just took a job. Just like before I went and got those work boots and on Monday morning I walked in. The first guy I saw I told him that Joe said to tell the foreman to put me to work. Just so happened the guy I was talking to was the foreman. Without asking any questions he put me to work right away. Wow, I couldn't believe it! It happened again. Was it God? No question, but was I willing to surrender to him? I couldn't see it. It's too much bitterness and anger and people I wanted to payback. Besides, God is good and I wasn't ...at least not now.

As always I suppressed that yearning, that feeling. Jeanne' was working in another part of the building. They had a good and easy job. She directed the recycle trucks to the spot where they would unload the recyclable waste. It was a good job and I had never asked what they did before.

Now I'm working and trying to forget the past. I could hardly wait to go back there and tell her. Just like that everything looked different for me. I had a purpose for living again. Now I'm going to have to see Joe and I was pretty confident he would be ok. Just as I thought, it was almost time to go home, I saw Joe. With a smile on his face he asked, "What are you doing here?" I said, "You told me to start today." He laughed and said, "I'll see you in the morning." Well! Things were looking up for me and at the same time Jeanne' and Larry was having problems with the company who was running the recycle center. Harley was having to come down from Seattle to talk to the head of the company, whose name was Ralph.doing this time, at some point I confronted Larry about what sherika told me.

I said a lot of things I shouldn't have said. I have no facts, his girlfriend was there and I let it all come out. Maybe I was wrong but from that time on I made his life and Jeanne' life a living hell as long as they were around me. More than that I wanted Larry back in Seattle , and right about now I didn't care if it were true or not, because shit like that should not have come up, not with him, Williams was hard enough.

So I declared war on the two of them. The way I acted at times, but we never fought. I guess Sherika may have been right. You can't fight the truth. After I was on the job a few weeks, Ralph had called Harley and ended that job with his company. Larry and Tanya didn't waste no time going back to Seattle.

Chapter 22

There's a Storm Brewing Inside of Me

Jeanne' in spite of my bitterness and anger wanted to stay with me. As long as I was sober we got along great or better. So we decided to start over again. We moved out of that apartment that Harley had gotten for them. This was fine with me as I wanted nothing to do with Harley or Larry and that place reminded me of them. Jeanne' found us a nice apartment in Clackamas County next to the mall. The apartments were brand new units. As long as we were moving forward I managed to stay sober (kind of) and that allowed me to want to make it work with her. The more comfortable I became with my surrounding the more I pushed her away it seemed. I didn't wake up in the morning saying, "Hey! You fucked over me." It wasn't' like that at all. I loved this girl and I think I really wanted it to work. Nevertheless, my pride wouldn't let the past go. All that anger and bitterness would begin to eat away at me and to make matters worse, my drinking became a problem once again, the more comfortable I became at work.

Going to work and coming home was a beautiful thing at times. All I had to do was think back to a few months ago. I was facing thirty (30) years and now here I am with a damn good job making nineteen (19) dollars and hour, living in this beautiful apartment with the girl I've always wanted. However, because of an encounter she had with William and now maybe Larry, I'm willing to blow it all. Man! I got so much going on inside of me.

I thought since I had survived the first few months I would be done with the anger and bitterness. Man! I thought back in Seattle I would have lost it then, but I got through that. So why now? I'm at a beautiful place in my life. For the first time in a long time I'm not running or scared of being caught by the police. This is a different kind of fight. I'm dealing with demons on the inside of me. They are telling me to get revenge. How do you fight against yourself? It seems Monday through Friday I was good. But Friday night, when I would start to drink this side would come out of me. I would start a fight with this girl by saying all kinds of nasty things to hurt her. Mainly saying the same ole shit, "You couldn't wait six months for me before you go and sleep with someone else," amongst other stupid comments. On Monday I would go back to work and think about all the things I said and truly I felt so ashamed. Then I would call her from work and tell her how sorry I am.

In the beginning I really was sorry. After apologizing I wouldn't do it for another three weeks or so. I could see that she was sorry that she had ever let herself go there with William, because she would tell me, "Herb, you can't go on like this," she would say, "Fight me, do whatever, but you can't go on like this." Lord knows I wanted to let go of the past, but I was too far gone. I wanted her to suffer for what she did. And at the same time she was missing the kids especially the boys. She also knew how much I loved those kids. Maybe she thought it'll take my mind off of the bullshit. She didn't waste any time going to get them and to my surprise it worked, but only for a while.

You see, the more comfortable I became on my job and with the city of Portland, the more I thought about what she did with those guys. I couldn't keep it inside of me any longer. The fights started up again, it went from just happening on the weekends to almost every day. It got so bad that the kids didn't want to be around me. In spite of the fights she wouldn't leave, but with the frame of mind I was in I knew it was hurting not only her but the kids. I didn't want the kids around me, not like this.

At this point I was filled with so much rage, anger and bitterness that I couldn't even think straight. One would think that I should be past all this by now, but I wasn't. I was just beginning. My mood would change out of the blue. For example, one day she was in the kitchen cooking and of course I was drinking a beer. The kids were having fun clowning around it was perfect, no fighting. All of a sudden something was said and everything changed for me. I turned into this angry person and caused a big fight and the kids were right in the middle of it. For the first time she called the police and needless to say I didn't want to listen to anyone because I felt I was the victim in the situation. I know that's crazy but that's how I saw it and I really saw it that way when I was drunk.

I really didn't want those kids around me like this and before I went to jail I wouldn't have done this around them. Now my true feelings are on the table, the kids know, Jeanne' knows now what am I going to do? The police are talking to me asking what happened. Jeanne' told them everything was alright until all of a sudden my anger swelled up inside me and I started a fight and I really didn't have an answer as to why. According to the police, in a situation like this one of us would have to leave and since she had the kids it was best if I left. I didn't want to leave but I couldn't be that lowdown to make her leave and take the kids somewhere. I'll be honest though, I had to think about it long and hard. In the end I realized the kids had nothing to do with this and uproot them after all of this drama was wrong so I just left. I stayed at a friend's house.

The next morning I came back and got dressed for work. While at work I thought about what happened the night before. I felt bad for the kids knowing how they felt about me in the beginning, them knowing how much I had loved their mother and now it had come to this. I decided that no matter what I was going through I did not want to hurt those kids. Well, after work I came home. I told her I really didn't have an answer for what I had done. She told me she wasn't looking for one. I was puzzled at this point because she and the kids both were in a really good mood considering what happened the night before. I thought when I came home I would get the cold shoulder not just Jeanne' but from the kids as well, but that doesn't seem to be the case.

I took their moods as a way of them showing me that no matter what was going on they were still going to be nice to me. Seeing this, I didn't push or even discuss the events of the night before and for the next couple of days I was fine.

I realized that I had fucked up big time because the kids were going back to live with their dad. Deep down inside I wanted them here with us but I knew I wasn't right. I was a complete mess. Maybe with them going back to Seattle I could get myself together and hopefully Jeanne' and I could be like we were in the beginning.

When she left to take the kids back to Seattle, I honestly didn't know if she would come back. On top of that I didn't know what I wanted and not only that my job was coming to an end. We were finishing up now. What am I going to do? Little did I know Joe was talking to Ralph about me staying on and running the plant. My job would be teaching worker's how to bail paper, sorting through paper and on the lines, operating the fork lift, the front end loader and everything in between. Here it is I am being given a second chance, an opportunity of a life time and at home I'm tripping. Something has to give and with so much on the line I decided to chill with the bullshit.

I'm glad I realized this because it wasn't long before Ralph wanted to meet with me about the job. When we met he basically told me he wanted me to be his right hand man. I was a part of the hiring process as well as training everyone that came into the warehouse. My job was to put the right people in the right place and train them to be the best. I was very honored and excited, to say the least, to be a part of something so big! This was just the break I needed. Maybe, just maybe this will be what helps to get me past what's eating me up inside. I accepted the job, of course.

I couldn't wait for Jeanne' to get back from Seattle so I could share the news with her, so I could tell her I was sorry and that I wanted her in my life forever. I only hoped she would forgive me for the stupid things I had done. I realized that in order for this to work I had to find out what is triggering all this anger inside of me. That's something I have to work on and it would have to start with forgiving and forgetting. When she returned from Seattle, I did all the things I knew she was used to me doing when things were good between us. In other words I was starting over.

In the months to come I worked hard on my relationship. Not only did I work on the relationship, but my job was important to me as well. Here I am training guys to operate the forklift, the baler, on the sorting line showing these guys what to keep and what to throw away...man it was all on me! I didn't shy away from this responsibility either. As a matter of fact, I embraced the responsibility that was given to me.

As time went on the recycle business in Portland grew very quickly. I had bales of paper stacked up to the ceiling, bales of soda cans ready to sell and not only was I busy in the warehouse Ralph also gave the responsibility to me to work with the brokers to sell this stuff. At this time in my life I wasn't going to church and I wasn't claiming to be a believer but there was no denying that this was the hand of God at work in my life. Life was good, I mean real good, I hardly drank at this point (that was a good thing) and the company was growing.

The growth of the company was a good thing and a bad thing at times. It was good because I made lots of money because of the hours and Ralph was the only person I answered to and he hardly came in the warehouse. The bad thing was that Ralph was hiring people in positions that weren't ready to be there because they didn't have the knowledge of what was going on. Some of the management positions that were being filled were with guys who were just given titles and eventually they became my supervisors. I didn't think this was right. In the beginning it was Ralph, the girls in the office and me. That's it. (I felt that) for him to look over me when it came to management positions was hurtful and I began to feel some resentment towards him and my job. I felt he was using me and had no intention of making this my warehouse.

It wasn't long before he proved me right. He hired his longtime friend Tom as the General Manager. Man, was I crushed. Ok, I didn't have the experience that Tom had but at the same time Tom didn't know this business. After working with Tom a while I was able to get past the fact that he was hired for the job. You see! As we worked together Tom made it quite clear that he felt that I should have gotten his job. Tom actually started to become like a father to me. Ralph however continued to bring these people on board. And for what?! Tom nor I knew why. He was the boss. To make matter worse most of these guys didn't want me in the position I had.

With all of this going on I began to hate my job. True to my nature I became that guy from a few month's ago. Jeanne' nor our relationship stood a chance. I dug up all the anger and bitterness from the past and added to it my current feelings about my job. How can things be going so well and then just fall apart? The only thing keeping me together was this job and the position I had. For things to be so uncomfortable at work made me feel uneasy and I was devastated. , how could he overlook me.

I was angry at work and at home and at this point. I would get angry about things at work and bring it home and take it out on Jeanne' although I knew I shouldn't. I would sometimes go for days without talking to her with no reason or explanation. Our relationship went downhill from here with no chance of getting better. I really didn't want it to get better. I never put my hands on her or anything it was all verbal and mental, but as she told me this was for her far worse than hitting her.

In my sick and twisted mind it felt good. I was not only betrayed by her but also by Ralph who was slowly taking away my job that I cared so much about. I had to get out what I was feeling and unfortunately it came out at home with her. The verbal and mental abuse had got so bad she finally moved back Seattle to get away from me and my anger and the drinking had started again.

In her absence I took to the clubs in the hood. I would find myself waking up in some chick's bed that I had just met the night before. This gave me some relief but I still had lots of anger and bitterness towards Ralph and Jeanne'. It just refused to go away. After hitting the clubs and sexing a different woman every weekend proved to go nowhere and solved nothing, I decided to get back on track and focus.

I started to accept my role at work as I had in the beginning.
I also started calling Jeanne'. I had a lot of work to do with
her. I said so many things that no one should say to anyone,
especially the person you are supposed to love. Knowing
this I knew it would take some time for her to come around.
I needed to ask myself was this what I wanted for myself. I
began to think maybe this is the best thing now. It was just
a few months ago when I wanted a fresh start and as soon
as something didn't go the way I wanted it to, I messed
things up. You know! I'm really starting to hate being sober.
It's so confusing. It seems like when I'm drinking, "It's fuck
everything and everybody." I know this really isn't reality,
the alcohol just makes it seem that way. See the problem
is I have been doing drugs and drinking so long that (fuck
everything and everybody) is the only mentality I knew and
felt comfortable with. I'm going to try to get myself together
starting with my girl and my job.

I knew it would be hard to submit to people I had no
respect for at work. There were way more than a few who
had gotten positions for reasons unknown to me (Ralph
had his reasons, I guess). It seemed the more business we
got the more bosses he hired and actually I really didn't fit
in anywhere but I was getting paid damn good money even
though my role was getting smaller and smaller. Despite

all the shady shit I felt Ralph was doing to me it seemed he needed me more and more. Since I have accepted things at work the way they are it's time to shift my focus to Jeanne'.

I need Jeanne' to come back to Portland. Underneath all the bullshit I was still a player at heart. I knew what turned her on and I knew just what to say and when to say it. It wasn't easy. Going back to Seattle the way she did, she must have felt ashamed and embarrassed. I'm sure my behavior made her think long and hard about coming back as well. I did the very things that her husband had done to her — putting her out and all the other dumb shit I was doing. Now I guess its kiss ass time. Flowers, calls, whatever it takes. I went one step further and decided to go up there on weekends. I knew her family would be pissed at me for the pain I cased her, but still in my mind I was a victim as well. I understood that they were concern but I felt that this was between the two of us so therefore I could care less about what they thought about me.

It took a few weekends of going up there but she was coming around. Eventually she moved back home. It felt so good to have her back and things were good at work too. All of this "feeling good" must've lasted about three (3) months. Ralph hit me with what he called a great opportunity. I was thinking, "What more can this fucker do to me." There was a night crew that cleaned up the place and he felt that the foreman wasn't doing his job. He thought I would be perfect for the position. That fucked me up big time and to make matters worse he didn't tell me one of the supervisor's told me (Hey Herb just play the game). I guess I was the only black on the job, I'm good. Naw, fuck that! I made this place what it is and these fuckers are trying to push me into the background. Maybe not out of the door but at least tucked away somewhere nice and neat. Well two can play this game. I took the job but with some conditions. First I wanted them to hire some blacks, Mexicans, etc. Well I began to really see what was going on.

No blacks, Mexicans nor any other races were hired after I took the job. I guess they thought I was enough. I began to push the issue and of course it didn't go over well with most of the foreman. After I constantly went to Ralph about it, I guess he felt he owed me that much and right away he hired some blacks and Mexicans but not through the company. He went to a temp agency. Man! This is really fucked up. Now I'm pissed off and back to being angry and bitter.

Well you know me I'm angry and bitter and somebody's gotta feel it so needless to say it wouldn't be too long before

I would tear down everything I was rebuilding with Jeanne'. I went back to drinking heavy. This was really not the time for me to be tripping. We had gotten a little three bedroom corner house in the northeast section of Portland and the kids were back with us. Somehow I let Ralph push the right button to set me off and as always I brought it home. One Friday night I got drunk for no reason and I started giving Jeanne' a lot of shit. It got pretty bad and before I knew it the police were at the front door and just like the first time I didn't want to hear anything.

I opened the door and let them in not knowing that Jeanne' had gotten a restraining order to keep me five hundred (500) feet away from her and the house. I couldn't believe it, then again I don't know why I couldn't believe it. Look at the shit I've done. I guess she had gotten the restraining order before it had gotten to this point and was just waiting on the right time. I didn't go to jail that night, mainly because I wasn't aware of the restraining order but I was asked to leave. I got my shit and there was nothing I could do. I went over to Cedric's house (a friend of ours) and hung out over there. Of course when I explained what happened it was all her fault. There were a few people over hanging out there as well including his cousin Shirley. We all hung out got fucked up and I ended up sleeping with Shirley. Over the next few days I ended up bouncing back and forth between Cedric and Shirley's houses. It was no secret where I was Cedric and Jimmy were the only friends we had in Portland. What I was doing wasn't a secret either. Jeanne' knew and seemingly didn't care. It didn't look like I was getting back into the house anytime soon and that really pissed me off.

Jeanne has the upper hand now having that damn restraining order. There was nothing for me to do but crash with Cedric and his family. It was cool in the beginning but once I sobered up and thought about all the bullshit I wanted back in my house. Jeanne was hell bent on teaching me a lesson though. I wasn't giving in not this time. I didn't like staying with someone else and actually it really felt like I was living out of my car. At work I was slacking and missing days or when I was there I was drunk or full of powder I got from the Mexican who was working with me. I ended up sharing everything that was going on with Tom and all I can say is, "Thank God for Tom."

The thought came to me to take off some time from work. I hate this job right now. I have no home to go to. A hurricane just went through Louisiana and it was the "Perfect Storm," an excuse for me to get away. I went to Tom about taking a leave of absence to get myself together as well as help my mother with the damage from the hurricane. Of course this was ok with Tom, so I took off three (3) months and headed for Louisiana.

Lord knows I was a mess and broken. Coming here I felt I could get myself together and this time for good. It was strange I mean really strange. Upon my arrival in Port Allen it felt different. I felt like a stranger for some reason and the first thing I saw was a new generation who had come on the scene. I mean I knew the parents of this new generation. Man! It was a sign of the times. My cousin Eric was the dope man and it was his time to shine. He had been in the shadow of Fat Cat and myself for a longtime from Port Allen to Compton. Now he has Port Allen all to himself and of course I was happy for him. I knew he wasn't going to hand me dope on a silver platter considering how I used to treat those guys. I knew he would make me work for whatever I wanted and I knew that and I welcomed it. If it was one thing I knew how to do that would be hustling. Looking at lil' cuz he had taken a little bit from me and a little bit from Fat Cat and put it all together and it was working for him.

It was no time to sit back and trip on Eric. I had come back to Port Allen to find myself (once again). I'm a hustler and since he was holding down Port Allen I would need

him because there were no checks coming in. One thing
I noticed about his game was that he had a lot of young
chicks hanging around him. This was mainly because of
this one young chick whom he was in love with. He had his
baby's momma (Tina) but this young girl was where his
heart wanted to be and Tina got bumped down to being
just his "baby momma." All this shit was crazy. I had enough
crazy shit going on in my life to know how that kind of shit
will bring you down.

As for me, somehow I was able to focus on me and I got
back into the dope game I loved so much. I recall him
giving me a little more than an eight ball and him telling
me something like you get one shot. Fuck this off and you
are on your own. My mind was made up, I wasn't going to
lose this time around. That eight ball turned into a quarter
ounce, the quarter ounce to a half ounce and a half ounce
into a whole damn ounce. I was rolling!

The tables turned quickly. Eric needed me. Why? In a
matter of weeks I was getting two or three ounces from
him every week. I picked up on one of the little chicks who
was hanging with his girlfriend. Just that quick I forgot all
about Jeanne'. It also seemed that the anger and bitterness
had gone away. I felt renewed in some way. Being around

those young chicks gave me a confidence I had been lacking for such a long time. I feel like my old self, things were moving so fast for me. I was loving every minute of it. There were times I wondered about my mom and what she was thinking but then again she was doing her own thing. The gambling boat had come to Louisiana and she and her sisters were deep into that, like everyone else in the Baton Rouge area. I don't think her opinion would have mattered to me anyway. When I'm into something I could care less about what anyone else thinks. Man! It wasn't too long before Georgia Ave. was off the chain and to be honest I didn't come back to Port Allen to do this.

It wasn't long before some family members expressed their dislike for the way I was doing business at the house and they were right. I was hurting when I came here and if this is the thing to get me back on track I was more than willing to have everyone angry at me as long as my mom didn't say anything I didn't care what anyone else said. The only thing I knew was that I wasn't hurting anymore and it's only been a matter of weeks and I was already seeing things differently.

I knew I had to go back to Portland, I knew that for sure. What I didn't know was — what was going to happen with Jeanne'? I had promised the chick who I was hanging with that she could be with me in Portland and that was a lie. I loved her hanging with me. I had a lot to prove to myself and going back to Portland and making it right was important to me. I wanted to prove to Jeanne' that I could bounce back from the past. In the meantime I'm loving being here in Port Allen having my way with this girl and other chicks I knew. I had a new outlook on life.

This new outlook forced me to see what Jeanne' did wasn't the end of the world after all. I didn't know what she was doing nor did I think about it. As of right now I'm doing me having money, young bitches life is good, but as always as soon as I get to a level of success I begin to use cocaine and those demons would follow. Just like in the beginning I would manage to use and sell but staying up for days at a time and this would take a toll on me. I kept my re-up money straight and that's all that mattered to me.

The cocaine use and the tension between family members was beginning to take its toll on me. There were times when I felt like that little kid in Sunrise who just wanted to be loved and in spite of the drugs and other bullshit there were nights when I would lay down to sleep, I would wake up in the middle of the night and all around my bed were angels. For the first few night I thought, I'm tripping from the dope," besides I'm staying up for days at a time. But I realized it was more than that it was real!

I remember one night everyone was gone and I was left alone and I wasn't high so I decided to get some sleep. My mom was gone to the boat and they had a scanner in the house to hear police activity and as I laid there, there appeared to be angels around my bed. Out of nowhere a voice said go check the scanner and I did. To my surprise the scanner was turned off. That scanner had not been off not since I had been here. C'mon! I knew I was wrong for selling dope out of my mom's house, but this was nothing new. I've done this before, but for someone to turn the scanner off was mind blowing to me. In the mean time I had to think and quick about what to do. I got the dope and went in the back yard. I put it in the ground and came back inside and turned the scanner back on. I laid down and began to think. There was no one around tonight. Usually there's all kinds of motherfuckers jocking me. Damn! Someone was trying to put me in jail tonight. But who?! Man! I didn't have a clue. Now I'm afraid of everybody — family, friends, everybody. It didn't matter who you were.

Once again it feels like it's me against the world. No doubt I was ready to take on anyone who came at me wrong. None of this bullshit would stop me at this point. I was winning and that was the only thing that mattered to me at this time. Also, I didn't feel like it was any pressure from the police, besides I wasn't here to stay. Still someone wanted me in jail or gone. I really knew this was the case when the scanner was turned off on another night. This time my mom had gone to Kansas City for the wedding of my sister, Bay. As always it was all kinds of niggas hanging out with me this night. While I'm kicking it with this girl, Eric and his crew, slowly everyone started to leave and before I knew it, it was me and one of my cousins left drinking and talking and then all of a sudden she had to go. I showed her to the door and said to myself maybe I should get some rest. I went to turn on the water in the shower. Before doing so I made sure the scanner was on. I went back into the bedroom to get my clothes for bed and then I went to take a shower. As I stood in the bathroom with the water running (ready to take a shower) like before a voice said to me, "Go back and check the scanner." I did what the voice said and just that fast the scanner was off. This freaked me out because I didn't hear anyone. Right then I ran and got the dope out of the bedroom and while the shower was still running I went outside to put the dope in the ground. I also looked around to see if I saw anything strange going on. Down the street I saw a tow truck parked on the street talking to someone. I went back in the house turned the shower off and got the fuck out of there.

I ran next door to the neighbor's house where they had a lot of flowers and rose bushes. I took my chances doing this because the police could have been staked out in those very bushes. I knew I was getting high on coke but I wasn't tripping I knew what I saw. After lying in those bushes a while I could see flashlights shining around in the back yard but no police came to the house that night. I tried to tell anybody who would listen what happened or what could have happened that night. My aunt and family members pushed it a side as to say this nigga is just high on that dope. I knew that it was time for me to go back to Portland, but I hadn't reached my goal and at the same time I couldn't get busted. I had to make a choice — leave now or risk my freedom. I chose to stay a little longer, just at least until my mother came back from Kansas City. I brought my concerns to her telling her what happened. Just like everyone else she down played it too. While I was sharing this with her I also told her about the angels I was seeing at night watching over me while I slept. Deep down inside I wanted her to believe me. Forget about the tow truck and the police scanner being turned off. I know that the angels are real. I said to her, "Mom there are angels in my room every night watching over me." She asked me, "How do you know that these are God's angels and not the devil?" I said, "Because when I'm lying there I feel peace and safety around me. It surpasses my understanding." She said, "Ok," and I said no more about the angels or the other occurrences.

In my heart I wondered did she believe me. I'd like to think she did. While I was thinking about this turn of events Tom (my boss) called. He was checking in on me since my leave of absence was coming to an end. He wanted to know if I was planning on coming back to work. I was glad to know I was wanted because here there were a few people who didn't want me around and it was so many people hanging around I couldn't figure out who and why. Considering what had happened in the past months I needed to go back and take another look at the job and Portland again. Maybe I should start over, I've done it before and this wouldn't be any different. Besides I'm always starting over. The question is what about Jeanne'. Will I let go of the past and make it work? After all she is holding down the fort while I'm gone. I've been sleeping with chicks and having a ball these last three months. I really won't have the answers to my questions until I get back and that's a few days away yet. In the meantime I'll try and make as much money as I can just as I had been doing these last three months.

I've come across some old friends some I hadn't seen in a long time and that was great for me it took me back to some good time and some not so good times. In a lot of ways this trip put things back into perspective because in the past I've always put pleasure before business. It has always led me to self-destruction. Now it's time to change that way of thinking and get my shit together for good. There's lots of questions I need to ask myself. Questions like: Do I accept my role at work and if so can I make the most of it or do I go on to something else? Most importantly — Is Jeanne' my future or do I move on? And last but not least — what do I do about my drinking? It is the root of all of my problems? (If it is) (Can I quit?) Maybe I can sort all of this out on the plane. One more thing — can I really do this alone? See back in Portland I don't have anyone to share these thoughts with. I've walked alone for so long I didn't think I'd ever need anybody, but as I get older, and I distance myself from the dope game I find life to be about people and with that comes having compassion, feeling, understanding, forgiveness, trust and last but not least <u>LOVE</u>.

In my crazy messed up world I knew nothing about living with these principles. My world is based on how much money and dope you have and that's it. I'm living in the real world now, I need this job, and they don't need me. I have come to realize that Jeanne' loved me in spite of me having her and Yolanda. On the plane I really thought about all of this. Upon my arrival in Portland I didn't wait until we left the airport before I started some shit. I guess one question was answered already. I hadn't' changed one bit when it came to her, but we made it through the weekend ok. The acid test will be Monday at work, would my attitude be the same or can I move forward. On the way there Monday morning, I'm having all kinds of mixed emotions. When I got there and looking at those same guys I had come to dislike right then I hated it and even more than before. I put on this front like everything was fine and I went about my business, but I wasn't happy at home the fussing and fighting picked up right where we left off and for the record it wasn't Jeanne'. She was kind, a true lady as always.

I was out of control I began to drink on my lunch break and almost every night me and some of the guys who work for me would go to the strip club and have lunch and of course watch the ladies dance. I had lost all respect for my relationship with Jeanne' and for my job. I felt like I was in quick sand and I was going down fast. To be honest I didn't want to feel this way because inside I wanted to make everything right, but there was something inside of me eating at me and I didn't know what to do about it. I drowned myself in self-pity. Drinking was the only way I knew to cope with this hurt or whatever it is that's eating away at me inside. Could it have been pride? The only thing I could think about was getting even, not willing to forgive or forget anyone who hurts me in any kind of way. Case in point! Just before I left for Louisiana a friend of mine and Jeanne' came down to Portland to find himself, get a job or whatever the case may have been. I didn't have a lot of time to kick it with him because I was leaving for Louisiana and I asked Jeanne' to look after him and give him a place to stay for a night or two if he needed it.

This was Tubby Cain. The first person to embrace me at the recycle center in Seattle. I called him friend. While I was in Louisiana he would come by the house occasionally I am told. That was ok but at some point he came at Jeanne' sexually. I don't know what he was thinking. I had never came at his girl Tina that way, but apparently Jeanne' had (come get it) written all over her face. Jeanne' waited until I got back to tell me this and needless to say with me already dealing with this job and my feelings about Jeanne' and drinking like a fish it wasn't what I needed to hear. At first I didn't know if I really gave a fuck but then this nigga was supposed to be my boy. He stayed at my crib and I stayed at his. Unlike William or maybe Larry I must confront him and no question it's going to be a fight. I hadn't heard from him since I've been back in town. I didn't know if he had left Portland and gone back to Seattle or what. So until I got a line on him the fight would have to wait. Besides I have enough shit going on in my life that I should just forgive him and forget it but I couldn't.

While I was gone Jeanne' had gotten a job at a supermarket and by now we only had one car. Since I made the most money I had the car. She really only wanted me to pick her up from work on the weekends. She rode the bus on the week days. Drowning in self-pity and drinking like a fish I was too drunk to pick her up but yet she continued to ask. There were a few times when I would go and pick her up. It meant a lot to her. I could see it in her eyes but for some reason I found doing little things like this hard to do. One night I was getting drunk with Cedric and Jimmy and I didn't go pick her up. She didn't call either, maybe she knew I was drunk and I wouldn't come. She didn't call but I didn't think twice about it. I mean she would just catch the bus. I heard a car pull up in front of the house and she walked up to the door telling somebody thanks for the ride. I didn't pay it much attention it was probably just a co-worker.

On another night she didn't call for me to pick her up. Just so happen I was outside putting out the trash or something and I see this caddy pull up and Jeanne' got out of the passenger side. I asked her about who was dropping her off. She told me it was a guy who had come in the store to shop often. and then my mind ran wild. Since she had the restraining order I was trying to play it cool but seeing the guy dropping off my girl wasn't' cool. It wasn't going to be long before I would confront her about this bullshit. When I confronted her we went back and forth about it. She insisted it was nothing more than a ride. But ever since this stuff with Williams I didn't fully trust her ass.

One night while sitting at the house getting drunk I made up my mind to confront this dude. The restraining order didn't matter to me at this point. This shit was going to stop and right now. On this night I waited standing on the street pacing up and down. The more I paced the crazier I got. When she and the dude pulled up I was out of my mind. I went walking towards the car and he stopped and she got out. I went off on her and then turned to check his ass. This cat didn't want no part of me. He had to see in my eyes I was ready to fuck somebody up. She played her hold card (the restraining order) and I went to jail. Because I was working I was placed in a program called Close Street. This program allowed you to sign yourself out as long as you stayed away from whatever it was that got you in jail. You just had to call in every day. I agreed but in my mind I wanted to do something. What? I didn't know, but it wasn't good.

Seeing that guy drop her off made me crazy and I knew she knew that. I let it get the best of me and like a damn fool I went by the house knowing it could cost me my job as well as my freedom. I knew better than to do this and like before I went and told Tom (my boss) what I was feeling. As always Tom was there for me. He begged me not to go over there, at least not right now. He said to give her some time to think. After all I've been rejecting her for such a long time. I listened to what he had to say but my mind was made up. I was determined to do something stupid.

I started missing days from work because I wanted to catch that nigga dropping her off one more time. I wanted to hurt this dude. I felt he had disrespected me because she knew I would be hanging around because Jimmy lived across the street from us and I had been hanging out there. I tried to talk to her and at times I thought she would let me back in. She would only talk to me from a distance. She was going by the restraining order at this time that was all I got. I was alright with that as long as dude kept his distance.

One night the caddy pulls up and I was totally fucked up. I came out of nowhere it must have seemed to them and as I walked to the driver's side of the car that dude saw me. He must have seen in my eyes I was going to do something stupid. Jeanne' got out of the car and took off running down the street. It seems like a second later the caddy burned rubber leaving. I went into the house full of rage and started breaking up anything in my sight. I knew the police would be coming so I had to make it quick. As I was leaving out the back door Jeanne' is outside with the police standing towards the front of the house. I don't think they knew if I was in the house or not, so I came out of that bitch running and I saw the cop turn around and look me in the eyes. I had a nice jump on him though. Having this hip replacement I knew I couldn't get far so I got into one of my neighbor's backyard a few houses away.

The neighbor had a couple of dogs and they began barking. The barking brought these people outside to see what was going on. As I'm hiding they ask me to leave but I couldn't go out there. I couldn't blame them though. I pleaded with them to let me stay hiding. They went back into the house. They didn't seem happy about it but they let me stay. I saw the police lights and the K-9 unit walking around. It was a good thing these people had dogs because this made it hard for the cops to know if it was me or the dogs that drew the k-9 dogs to the house. My only chance was these people not giving me up and thank God they didn't. As soon as the police left they made me leave.

I made my way to Shirley's house. I'm safe for the time being. I make myself comfortable and little did Shirley know she was going to be my alibi. It was perfect. She and some chick was getting high on crack but I didn't care what she was into. I just needed to look normal and not like I was hiding from the police. I kicked back and started talking to them. It wasn't long before Shirley sent home girl on her way. I knew how much she wanted me and she was going to have me every chance she got. I was cool with that. Matter of fact there were other chicks I had like that. The next day I was hung over and trying to gather my thoughts. First I had to get the fuck out of Shirley's house before Jeanne' heard about it. Jeanne' hated this chick for this very reason. If she found out I knew I wouldn't have a chance at talking to her. I went to Cedric's house and tell him everything. Like Tom, Cedric is a true friend. He tells me to just chill out with him and when Jeanne' gets off work he'll go see her on my behalf. At this point all I could do was wait to see what she would say to Cedric. I've fucked up this time and now going into the house breaking shit up — I'm going to jail for sure.

Cedric came back from visiting Jeanne' and just as I thought she's pissed. She's sick of my shit and I can't blame her. I went too far this time. Well there goes my job and everything else I've worked for. I don't have an answer for any of this. My actions were totally out of line both at home and at work.

I'm feeling like a prisoner in my own mind again. I thought I hated Jeanne' and my job. But after all of this I realized that Jeanne' and my job was my foundation. One day I'm chilling at Cedric's crib. The phone rings and Pam, Cedric's wife said, "It's for you." I said to myself it's Jeanne' and maybe there's hope after all. Wrong! This guy tells me, "Look out of the window." Wow! It's the police, three cars maybe and no telling where else they are posted up. The first officer I saw was the one who chased me the night of my escape. I later found out from Cedric that he was well known in the hood. They called him "Super Cop." I guess he thought he was some kind of bad ass. Well, it's over for me. I'm going to jail. There's no running this time and the only thing to do now is to go outside and face the music. And that's exactly what I did.

www.ingramcontent.com/pod-product-compliance
Lightning Source LLC
Chambersburg PA
CBHW060011100426
42740CB00010B/1451